Curriculum Policy

A Reader edited by

ROB MOORE

and

JENNY OZGA

at the Open University

PERGAMON PRESS

Member of Maxwell Macmillan Pergamon Publishing Corporation

OXFORD • NEW YORK • BEIJING • FRANKFURT
SÃO PAULO • SYDNEY • TOKYO • TORONTO
in association with

THE OPEN UNIVERSITY

U.K.

Pergamon Press plc, Headington Hill Hall
Oxford OX3 0BW, England

U.S.A.

Pergamon Press, Inc., Maxwell House, Fairview Park,
Elmsford, New York 10523, U.S.A.

PEOPLE'S REPUBLIC
OF CHINA

Pergamon Press, Room 4037, Qianmen Hotel, Beijing,
People's Republic of China

FEDERAL REPUBLIC
OF GERMANY

Pergamon Press GmbH, Hammerweg 6,
D-6242 Kronberg, Federal Republic of Germany

BRAZIL

Pergamon Editora Ltda, Rua Eça de Queiros, 346
CEP 04011, Paraiso, São Paulo, Brazil

AUSTRALIA

Pergamon Press (Australia) Pty Ltd., PO Box 544,
Potts Point, NSW 2011, Australia

JAPAN

Pergamon Press, 5th Floor, Matsuoka Central Building,
1-7-1 Nishishinjuku, Shinjuku-ku, Tokyo 160, Japan

CANADA

Pergamon Press Canada Ltd, Suite No 271,
253 College Street, Toronto, Ontario, Canada M5T 1R5

Selection and Editorial Material Copyright © 1991 The
Open University

First edition 1991

Library of Congress Cataloging in Publication Data
Curriculum policy: a reader/edited by Rob Moore and
Jenny Ozga.
p.   cm.
1. Education—Great Britain—Curricula.   2. Education
and state—Great Britain.   I. Moore, Rob.   II. Ozga,
Jennifer.
LB1564. G7C875   1990   375'.00941—dc20   90-46230

British Library Cataloguing in Publication Data
Moore, Rob
Curriculum policy.
1. Great Britain. Schools. Curriculum
I. Title   II. Ozga, Jennifer   III. Open University
375.00941

ISBN 0-08-041022-7 Hard cover
ISBN 0-08-040818-4 Flexicover

Printed in Great Britain by BPCC Wheatons Ltd, Exeter

Curriculum Policy

This reader is one part of an Open University integrated teaching system and the selection is therefore related to other material available to students. It is designed to evoke the critical understanding of students. Opinions expressed in it are not necessarily those of the course team or of the University.

Preface

This reader consists of a collection of articles which form part of the Open University course E333, Policy-making in Education. The course critically examines ways of analysing education policy, discusses the structure and process of education policy-making in central and local government, and analyses education policy in practice through case studies of particular policy issues.

The primary concern of this reader is with policy in relation to the curriculum. Because the reader forms only one part of the course (much of which consists of written texts or broadcasts discussing issues raised in the reader articles), it cannot claim to offer a complete picture of education policy-making in relation to the curriculum. The selection of articles has been made with the overall course content in mind. It has been designed to highlight specific problems, and to develop students' critical understanding. Opinions expressed within articles are, therefore, not necessarily those of the course team nor of the university. However, the editors believe that the selection, though not comprehensive, focuses on major issues and will be useful to anyone with an interest in the area.

There are three other readers, also published by Pergamon Press, and related to case studies of education policy which are discussed in course material. These readers are:

Policy-making in Education: the breakdown of consensus. Edited by I. McNay and J. Ozga.

Race and Gender: Equal opportunity policies in education. Edited by M. Arnot.

Education, Training and Employment: towards a new vocationalism? Edited by R. Dale.

It is not necessary to become an undergraduate of the Open University in order to stay the course of which this reader is part. Further information about the course associated with this book may be obtained by writing to: The Admissions Office, The Open University, P.O. Box 48, Walton Hall, Milton Keynes, MK7 6AA.

Contents

1

Introduction

THE LAST decade has seen an unprecedented amount of activity in curriculum policy, and recent years have seen the putting in place of elaborate mechanisms which legislate for the content of the curriculum and establish procedures through which the delivery of that content is tested. It has become commonplace to contrast this activity in the curriculum area, and the manner of its delivery through the Education Reform Act, with the preceding period of teacher and LEA autonomy in curricular matters, and the legislation, in the 1944 and 1945 Education Acts, that underpinned that.

We have a number of concerns in this reader and in the course material associated with it. One of them is to explore the reasons for the growth of policy activity in the curriculum in recent years. Another related topic is the issue of why that activity took the form that it did, while a third topic for exploration concerns the coherence of policy for the curriculum. All of these issues are contentious, all of them could provoke different responses.

Furthermore, there are other areas which demand attention—the implications of particular curriculum policies for teachers and LEAs, for example, or the view of teaching and learning which particular curriculum policies enshrine, implicitly or explicitly. It should, therefore, be readily apparent that this collection cannot be comprehensive. It is a selection which reflects, first and foremost, the concerns of the course of which it forms part. But it is also, we hope, a coherent attempt to address some of the more complex ideas and debates surrounding curriculum policy. One of the major concerns of the course is with attempting to develop analysis rather than description, and this is a balance of priorities also reflected in the reader. We have divided it into three parts, the first gives the immediate background to recent curriculum policy, including as it does Hough's discussion of increasing concern about the need to link education to economic growth, and curriculum to the needs of industry. That part also includes Kirk's comprehensive review of policy developments indicating greater central control of the curriculum up to and including the Education Reform Act of 1988. The second part looks at a variety of ways of constructing the curriculum, all of which have had an impact on policy. This is not a comprehensive review of positions, nor do we want to suggest that by including them we endorse any of them, the selection is related to the discussion in the course text. However, it does cover a range of very different and significant positions, from the FEU's technical distinctions between objectives and process models, through Mathieson and Bernbaum's tracing of the origins of academic conservatism in English education, to Bailey's discussion of the merits of liberal education. Scruton's piece is an attack on multi-culturalism and a statement of the uses of curriculum as a bastion and transmitter of 'English' culture, an influential position in relation to the discussion of the kind of history to be offered in the National Curriculum.

Part 3 of the reader offers a series of critiques of current policy (although it should be said that the divisions between parts are not watertight, there are implicit and explicit critiques in Part 2). However, this section is concerned with the immediate impact of the ERA, and especially of the National Curriculum and Assessment proposals. Jones looks at the origins of some of the Act's proposals, and in particular at the contradictory nature of much current curriculum and assessment policy, which he interprets as reflecting the different priorities of different groups contributing to policy. Whitty examines the major contradiction in the Act between increased state control, especially of curriculum, and the opening of the system to the vagaries of the market and individual choice, while the collection is concluded by Ahier's study of some of the unintended consequences of closer industry-education links. This brief review of contents should make the rationale for their selection apparent, though, of course, that rationale is only fully developed in the course text. We hope it is clear that we wanted to review the immediate history of policy for the curriculum in such a way as to remind readers of the main issues, and from there to look at some of the key ideas which have contributed to how we define the curriculum, and what we expect it to do. It should be apparent that those definitions are intensely political, and that some of them set up strong opposition in others—Bailey's liberal education sits unhappily with the vocationalist aims of the conservative modernizers, to take but one example. The readings address different issues, ranging from the immediate causes of concern about the curriculum among policy-makers, to different ways of constructing the curriculum, to discussion of some of the apparent contradictions in current policy. As this is a source book, we have let the selection speak for itself, believing that one of the principal lessons to be drawn from the study of the curriculum, as from the study of other policy issues in education is that interpretation depends on the perspective adopted, and the variety of perspectives on curriculum policy is bewilderingly evident at present. However, there are some general points about curriculum policy that we would like to make here.

Firstly, we need to take account of a wide range of activity when studying curriculum policy, and not simply focus on the provisions of the National Curriculum, or the content of the Action Plan, and the details of assessment procedures. They are self-evidently part of curriculum policy, as are initiatives which derive from the impact of vocationalism on education. But there are other policies which affect curriculum, these include the level of resource available for initiatives, ways of delivering that resource, and the structure of school provision. The impact of the ERA in those areas will have an effect on curriculum; the effects of LMS are already making themselves felt in areas unprotected by the national curriculum, such as music, and we do not know, at the time of compiling this collection, the likely future of Grant Maintained Schools. If they become fairly widespread, and if the City Technology Colleges are successful and affect intake to and the curriculum of existing local schools, then the impact of ERA on the structure of provision will be profound, and we may well see the emergence of differentiated schools with very different types of curriculum. Those issues, then, are curriculum policy issues.

Less structural, more diffuse issues concerning definitions of useful or appropriate knowledge are also curriculum policy issues; curriculum policies carry within them a view of what is appropriate to be learned in school. Behind those views lie beliefs about what education is for, beliefs which are hotly contested, and are polarized between those who think that education should serve the needs of the nation, and those who see it as primarily concerned with the fulfilment of individual potential. There are many positions between these polarities, and, of course, there are those who argue that the national interest serves the best interests of the individual. All curriculum policies carry within them a view of what should be learned, and thus of the purpose of education. These issues, then, which might be categorized as philosophical, are also policy issues.

It is perhaps the case that different views about what should be taught underlie the apparently contradictory nature of current developments in curriculum policy, where we see a vocationalist element working through TVE1 and related initiatives, and a traditional element defending academic subjects in the National Curriculum, while the progressives have found themselves either excluded from the process of policy change or welcoming only parts of it—the development of profiling, for example. The complexities are much greater than this simple division suggests, the labels progressive, traditionalist, and vocationalist suggest neat divisions which are not to be found in the real world, where people hold apparently contradictory positions. In relation to the curriculum, there is the further problem that some of the most active proponents of curriculum reform are opposed to the manner in which that reform is being delivered, as committed Neo-Liberals, opposed to state intervention, they strongly disapprove of a centrally-imposed and monitored national curriculum (see both the Jones and Whitty chapters for further discussion of this point).

Our view of the curriculum, and of what constitutes curriculum policy, is a broad one, and is not confined to enquiry into the distribution of time for selected subjects in a school timetable. The broad view, of course, raises a considerable number of complex issues, as it is probably in the arena of curriculum policy that differences of opinion about policy, different economic and political pressures, and the weight of different historical traditions become most apparent. In considering those items, it may be helpful to look at arguments for reform in more detail.

These arguments would include:

—the need to modernize the curriculum and make it relevant to the needs of the economy
—the need to allow greater consumer choice (consumers here include parents and representatives of the community, especially the business community)
—the need to improve quality, and to raise standards
—the need to reassert the 'national' culture
—the need to re-establish appropriate i.e. Christian and traditional familiar values; and values supportive of enterprise and industry
—the need to revive the traditional academic curriculum.

Other arguments which contributed to the upsurge of activity in curriculum policy concern the need to do something about high youth unemployment in the 1980s, and the attack on 'producer capture' which manifested itself in this context in the reduction of LEA autonomy, and of professional control over curriculum and examinations. (Kirk's chapter provides the details). The attack on 'producer capture' was, of course, principally aimed at teachers, and curriculum policy should not be seen in isolation from policy related to teachers. Here there are a number of relevant policy developments, including the introduction of the contract in England and Wales in 1987, the restructuring of the teaching work-force that accompanied it, as well as policies relating to teacher supply and training.

This broad conception of what the curriculum is about reflects our concern to locate curriculum issues within the wider context of the public and political debates which lie behind policy construction rather than within the more conventional educationalist frameworks (such as theories of how children learn). An integral feature of the educational reforms of the eighties has been the objective of opening up the curriculum to a broader, non-professional range of public constituencies (consumers, employers, politicians). Consequently, teachers are having to take account of the demands and expectations of groups previously excluded from 'the secret garden of the curriculum'. Although, at one level, these constituencies are defined, atomistically, as 'consumers', at another they are invoked, appealed to and, crucially, constructed within the ideological discourse of political and media dispute.

A distinctive feature of the past decade has been the way in which educational issues have been incorporated into a wider political debate and have been used to construct a political agenda in which disputes about what constitutes 'citizenship' have been a primary concern. This is reflected, for instance, in the 'modernizer's' argument which attributes economic decline to the effects of liberal-humanism and which promotes the 'enterprise culture' as part of the solution. This attack upon liberal education is linked to the more general attack upon 'the liberal establishment' and 'the chattering classes'. It promotes the model of the aggressive, enterprising entrepreneur against that of the liberally educated person in either its conservative 'gentlemanly' or 'trendy-lefty' form. At the same time, the neo-conservatives have attacked 'educational theorists' for promoting curriculum interests, such as multicultural or anti-sexist education, which are seen as undermining traditional values, social roles and respect for authority. Hence, rather than education as such being a 'political issue' (as with earlier debates around comprehensivization), education has been incorporated within a political discourse serving much broader ideological interests.

What these public and ideological debates around the curriculum reveal is the way in which thinking about education is a way of thinking about society at large. The public debates are constructed around accounts of what our society is currently like—in particular its weaknesses and problems. Although these concerns are most obviously expressed in relation to areas such as 'race', gender and sexuality, it is equally true for the long-standing debate about the virtues of 'traditional' versus 'progressive' education and public concerns around discipline and standards. The teachers' professional concern with 'how children learn' is translated, within the public debate, into a discourse about society and its citizens. Hence, press coverage of the debate around history in the National Curriculum has focused, almost exclusively, upon competing ways in which the national 'story' should be told and what it *means* to *be* British.

The selections in this reader have been chosen, in part, for the ways in which they tell such 'stories'. Their significance lies not just in the kinds of accounts which they provide, but also in 'the way they tell it'. Their styles are as symptomatic as their content. Hence, the FEU extract typifies a particular 'technicist' presentation which constructs a contrast between educational ideologies according to criteria which differ radically from those employed by the liberal, Charles Bailey, for instance. Although the various pieces tend to be addressing the same basic dichotomy within educational ideologies, they construct that opposition and define the salient features of each position in quite different ways. Ahier's piece critically examines processes which are common to most of these accounts, in particular their tendency to simplify cultural and institutional linkages and processes within and between education and the wider society.

Inevitably, if often implicitly, such 'stories' must entail assumptions about 'social causality'—about how education can affect society in order to produce the effects attributed to it. Educationalists have traditionally supported positive accounts of such causal relationships. Human Capi⫟

theory, for example, provided a major justification for the educational expansion of the fifties and sixties by presenting investment in education as an investment in national economic growth and prosperity. The 'stories' which lie behind current reforms cast education, and the teaching profession, in a very different role. The most immediate consequence of this, for teachers, is their marginalization within the new institutional arrangements for controlling education.

The connection between policy towards the teaching force and curriculum policy is an interesting theme to pursue historically, and a historical perspective on the current reform process is essential. It enables us to see that conflict over what should be taught, and what is appropriate knowledge is not new. The growth of state provision of education may be understood to a large extent as the story of tension and conflict, as policy-makers struggled to retain a stratified and differentiated system, in which appropriate knowledge was defined according to class, against the growing demand for access to education which was more than rudimentary preparation for labour. The differentiated structure, with public schools at the top and elementary schools at the bottom, was consistently challenged by egalitarian demands for the fulfilment of potential, allied to human capital theory's emphasis on exploiting talent. The differentiated system contained in the 1944 and 1945 education acts was eroded by these arguments, as was the differentiated curriculum. To return to the point about policy for teachers and policy for the curriculum running together, it is interesting that in earlier periods of strong central control over content, especially that following the Revised Code of 1862, there was also strong central control over teacher training and supply, and inspection and testing of teachers' work. From this followed a decline in the status of most teachers. The period of greatest teacher influence, the 1960s, is also a period of increased teacher influence on the curriculum, increased teacher status and autonomy.

One interpretation of current curriculum policy points to historical precedent to conclude that current policy is primarily intended to reintroduce or reassert a differentiated curriculum and structure of provision, with the distinction between training and education reflected in the differences between state and Grant Maintained Schools.

That interpretation rests on a particular perspective, and there are, of course, competing perspectives, most obviously those of the Neo-Liberals/ New Right which are articulated in the policies themselves. We are still in the pr   ss of change, which makes interpretation difficult, but it is, e   dependent on perspective.

Part 1

Background

2

Education and the National Economy

J. R. HOUGH*

The Education System

There have been many attempts to attribute blame or responsibility for Britain's industrial decline. Scapegoats have included, perhaps not surprisingly, both trade unions and management, or the social class system has been seen to be at fault. The country's education system, too, has not escaped criticism. Over a long period of years there have developed allegations that schools and colleges, and even polytechnics and universities, were paying insufficient attention to the needs of the economy in general and of industry in particular and were even guilty of inculcating anti-industrial attitudes. Young people emerged from the education system, it was alleged, determined if at all possible not to work in industry or, as the argument was sometimes cited, 'not to get their hands dirty'.

The notion of a direct and crucial relationship between the national economy and the output of the education system has received much attention over the last two years or so. It was referred to in the White Paper *Better Schools*[1] published in March 1985 and was the dominant theme throughout the Green Paper *The Development of Higher Education into the 1990s*[2] published in May that year. Commentary on such a relationship has a long history. It was referred to by the early economists in the nineteenth century and figured in publications relating to education throughout the first half of the twentieth century. The rapid growth of education after 1945 led on to the perceived need for a series of official reports covering different aspects of the education system, and one aspect referred to in each of these reports was the connection with the needs of industry and of the national economy.

It has to be remembered that education in Britain, perhaps influenced by the public school tradition and by nineteenth-century notions of a 'Classical

*Source: From Hough, J. R. (1987) *Education and the National Economy*, pp. 8–26, Croom Helm, London.

9

Education', has always sought to have a wide focus and to educate 'the whole child' with all that that implied in terms of the development of cultural, literary, and aesthetic awareness (even leading on in more recent times to the notion of 'education for leisure'): such emphasis needed to be set alongside notions of the economic dimension to the education the pupils received, as was clearly recognized by the first of the major reports in question, the Crowther Report:[3]

> The task of education in the technological age is thus a double one. On the one hand, there is a duty to set young people on the road to acquiring the bewildering variety of qualifications they will need to earn their living. On the other hand, running through and across these vocational purposes, there is also a duty to remember those other objectives of any education, which have little or nothing to do with vocation, but are concerned with the development of human personality and with teaching the individual to see himself in due proportion to the world in which he has been set . . . we have tried not to lose sight of the economic and vocational purposes that an effective educational system should serve. But children are not the 'supply' that meets any 'demand' however urgent. They are individual human beings, and the primary concern of the schools should not be with the living they will earn but with the life they will lead (Crowther Report, 1959).

It was perhaps significant that this report covered school pupils in the age group 15 to 18 and had much to say about the economy and about economic change, although as will be seen this was more from the standpoint of the pupils than in terms of the needs of industry:

> Of all the driving forces of change in the present day, among the strongest are those that show up in economic form, those that bear . . . upon the living the pupils in the schools are looking forward to being able to earn.
> Since a high level of national productivity can only be sustained by brains and skill, the schools have a higher challenge to meet.
> It is now (or should be) apparent to all that education pays, always in the long run, and often quite quickly.
> Not only have there been plenty of jobs for the qualified, there has been a steadily growing list of desirable callings that cannot be entered without a qualification.
> The other great force . . . that is transforming the role of education is the rising importance of being properly qualified.
> Qualifications have always been required for the professions. What has been happening in the last twenty years is that the same requirement has been spreading over a much larger field of employment (Crowther Report, 1959).

The report went on to revert to the dual theme cited previously:

> In this report, we have made no attempt to disentangle (the) two purposes of education. Both are worthy and compelling and we accept them both. Primacy must be given to the human rights of the individual boy or girl. But we do not believe that the pursuit of national efficiency can be ranked much lower. . . . If (education) be regarded as a social service, as part of the 'condition of the people', there seems to us to be no social injustice in our community at the present time more loudly crying out for reform than the condition in which scores of thousands of our children are released into the labour market. If it be regarded as an investment in national efficiency, we find it difficult to conceive that there could be any other application of money giving a larger or more certain return in the quickening of enterprise, in the stimulation of invention or in the general sharpening of those wits by which alone a trading nation in a crowded island can hope to make its living (Crowther Report, 1959).

These extracts have been quoted at some length because they show clearly that concern over the relationship between education and the economy, which has received much public attention in recent years, is neither very new nor very original. Over twenty-five years ago it was articulated at length but whereas other aspects of the Crowther Report—such as the raising of the school-leaving age—were immediately seized on and became the focus for major issues of educational policy, this particular aspect passed comparatively unnoticed. Worries over Britain's deteriorating economic performance had not in 1959 come to achieve such predominance as they were to do subsequently and it is therefore understandable that this aspect received much less attention in the report, as the above extracts indicate, than the future careers and livelihoods of the young people with whom the report was concerned. The authors of the report felt, as is clear from the above extracts, that they should not go on to assess whether more (or fewer) scientists and technologists would be needed in the future but they do seem to have suspected that if there were to be a problem over the numbers so qualified, far from there being a deficit there could even be a surplus.

One other question referred to in the above extracts and developed at length elsewhere in the Crowther Report, namely the use by employers of educational certificates as a filtering mechanism when recruiting staff even when the subjects studied have no direct connection with the work to be done, subsequently received much attention under the title 'the screening hypothesis'. This is, as we shall see, closely related to the view of educational qualifications as a screening or filter mechanism facilitating the task of employers in choosing young people for employment situations, even when the subjects studied have little or no direct relevance to the work in question.

Only a year and a half after Crowther the government of the day felt the need for another major study, this time of 'the education of pupils aged 13 to 16 of average and less than average ability' and therefore overlapping considerably with it: the Newsom Report, *Half Our Future*,[4] was published in 1963 and it had no doubts as to the nation's requirements for technically qualified personnel:

> The progress of automation and the application of other technological developments are likely to be delayed by lack of trained personnel. . . . It remains doubtful whether the number of new entrants into skilled occupations will be sufficient to match future needs (Newsom Report, 1963).

(the last sentence being quoted with approval from the 1962 White Paper on Industrial Training). Newsom recommended the extension of practical work-experience and of 'Introduction to Industry' type courses but in general concentrated on matters within schools and had rather little to say about links between education and the world of work, possibly because it did not wish to overlap with the work of Crowther.

In the same year, 1963, came the report[5] which is now seen in retrospect as the cornerstone on which the subsequent mushrooming of higher education in Britain was based. The Robbins Committee was set up not by the Minister of Education but by the Prime Minister and its report emanated not from the Ministry of Education but from the Treasury and was presented directly to Parliament as a Command paper: its status was therefore virtually assured in advance. The oft-cited main principle embodied in the Robbins Report, that:

> courses of higher education should be available for all those who are qualified by ability and attainment to pursue them and who wish to do so (Robbins Report, 1963).

was seen by the authors as being directly, although by no means solely, related to economic and vocational needs, whether or not the courses in question imparted specifically vocationally-relevant or technical skills. A companion recommendation, which has received much less subsequent publicity, was that the future growth of degree-level education (then concentrated almost entirely in universities) should embrace:

> some further increase beyond 51 per cent in the proportion of students taking science and technology (Robbins Report, 1963).

In reaching this conclusion the Committee was apparently influenced partly by evidence of general vocational trends, partly by statistics showing that from 1958 onwards A-level passes in mathematics and science had been increasing more slowly than those in the non-science subjects, and partly by such views as

> developments in science are increasingly a part of daily life

and

> a science course, whether pure or applied, can make as valid a contribution to general education as any other (Robbins Report 1963).

The concept of a need to aid the re-direction of students towards science and technology does not sit easily with the UK educational system's traditional reliance, at least at the level of post-compulsory education, on the 'Social Demand' approach, i.e. provided students are qualified (usually via appropriate passes at GCE A-level) to take a degree-level course of study they should be able to choose the subject area in which they wish to specialize, almost without restriction.

The theme of needing to have more students in the fields of science and technology was to be taken up in detail by an official report commissioned just two years after Robbins and published in 1968. Any student of educational developments during the years in question should have at least an outline knowledge of the place and significance of the Crowther, Newsom and Robbins Reports. Which of them will have even heard of the Dainton Report,[6] let alone know anything of its content or recommendations? Perhaps the subsequent obscurity of this report, which was entitled *Enquiry into the Flow of Candidates in Science and Technology into Higher Education,* signifies the lack of public interest in what it had to say and may therefore be taken as symptomatic of the alleged gulf that was opening up between educational development and national economic need? Be that as it may, the views of the small Dainton Committee, which had only six members, make powerful reading:

> the implications of the swing from science are far-reaching. Foremost, for scientific man-power policy, is the prospect of a pause in the growth of new supply to the stock of qualified scientists and technologists. . . . In relation to the educational system our findings suggest a conflict between patterns of personal preferences and social aspirations (working against the traditional sciences) and published evidence as to the demand for more scientists and technologists. . . . Tighter competition for newly qualified manpower in the early 1970s could have restrictive effects on new developments dependent on graduates in specialized fields (Dainton Report, 1968).

Attempts by the Dainton Committee to diagnose the cause of the drift away from science and technology at degree level focused on reactions to the study of scientific subjects in schools, reactions summarized in unattractive terms:

> some pupils . . . are deterred by the apparent rigour and unattractiveness of science
>
> most young people are now able to choose apparently less rigorous alternatives
>
> scientific studies in schools may be suffering from the after-effects of the intense competition for university places in science and technology which characterized the 1950s
>
> for many young people science, engineering and technology seem out of touch with human and social affairs
>
> the objectivity of science and the purposefulness of technology have become identified, for some, with insensitivity and indifference
>
> there are indisputable signs of an acute shortage of graduate scientists in schools at present, particularly in mathematics, in the intensive use of science and mathematics graduate teachers in schools compared with those in other disciplines, and in the extent to which these subjects are taught by teachers whose main subject of qualification is in other fields (Dainton Report, 1968).

The fate of the Dainton Report may be summarized by noting that its main conclusion:

> We recommend a broad span of studies in the sixth forms of schools; and that, in consequence, irreversible decisions for or against science, engineering and technology, be postponed as late as possible (Dainton Report, 1968).

was never acted upon, indeed was completely ignored, before eventually being resurrected in another guise some fifteen years later.

And finally, in this consideration of official reports relating to education, rather briefer reference may be made to the Russell Report.[7] The Russell Committee, in what seem as curiously restrictive terms of reference, was set up to enquire into 'non-vocational adult education' but that the Committee did not feel narrowly bound by this brief is shown, for example, by the fact that one whole section of the report was devoted to 'Adult Education in Relation to Industry': here and elsewhere the report emphasized the trends already noted above, viz. towards more skilled working and towards regular updating and acquisition of new skills during a time of rapid technological change. Adult Education as traditionally defined in the UK was, however, seen by implication as making only a marginal contribution towards the fulfilment of such needs.

Continuing Criticism and the 'Great Debate'

Criticism of the educational system and its economic role has continued. An early and influential critic could write:

> So far from there being a close relationship between what the schools attempt to do and what industry requires, indeed, there have in the past been strong influences against vocational education, at any rate until after the secondary stage (Carter 1966).[8]

and such accusations continued intermittently in subsequent years. With the 'Great Debate' initiated by Prime Minister James Callaghan in 1976 this question came once more into prominence. Speaking at Ruskin College, Oxford, in October, Mr Callaghan detailed at some length the alleged shortcomings, largely from industry's point of view, of the education that children and young people were receiving, at all levels:

> I am concerned on my journeys to find complaints from industry that new recruits from the schools sometimes do not have the basic tools to do the job that is required.
> I have been concerned to find that many of our best trained students who have completed the higher levels of education at university or polytechnic have no desire or intention of joining industry. Their preferences are to stay in academic life (very pleasant, I know) or to find their way into the civil service. There seems to be a need for a more technological bias in science teaching that will lead towards practical applications in industry rather than towards academic studies.
> Or, to take other examples, why is it, as I am told, that such a high proportion of girls abandon science before they leave school? Then there is concern about the standards of numeracy of school leavers. Is there not a case for a professional review of the mathematics needed by industry at different levels? To what extent are these deficiencies the result of insufficient co-ordination between schools and industry? Indeed how much of the criticism about the absence of basic skills and attitudes is due to industry's own shortcomings rather than to the education system? Why is it that 30,000 vacancies for students in science and engineering in our universities and polytechnics were not taken up last year while the humanities courses were full? . . . There is no virtue in producing socially well adjusted members of society who are unemployed because they do not have the skills. Nor at the other extreme must they be technically efficient robots (*The Times Education Supplement*, 22 October, 1976).[9]

Much the same theme was repeated by the government in the Green Paper *Education in Schools* issued the following year:

> The Prime Minister's concern about the relevance of present-day education to the needs of industry and commerce was reflected in many of the comments about this aspect of schools education at the regional conferences. It was said that the school system is geared to promote the importance of academic learning and careers with the result that pupils, especially the more able, are prejudiced against work in productive industry and trade; that teachers lack experience, knowledge and understanding of trade and industry; that curricula are not related to the realities of most pupils' work after leaving school; and that pupils leave school with little or no understanding of the workings, or importance, of the wealth-producing sector of our economy (Green Paper, 1977)[10]

The 1985 Green Paper

It was, however, as indicated previously, in 1985 that the question of a crucial relationship between economic performance and the country's education system came once again into prominence with the publication, within two months of each other, of the White Paper *Better Schools* and the Green Paper *The Development of Higher Education into the 1990s*. The former included various references to this relationship on the lines of: 'pupils need to have acquired, far more than at present, the qualities and skills required for work in a technological age'. Throughout the Green Paper, however, this theme appears in every section and may be said to be the dominant idea that the Green Paper expressed—indeed much of the criticism subsequently directed at the Green Paper suggested that it had gone too far in that direction, to the neglect of other priorities.

The following extracts will serve to indicate the flavour of the Green Paper's emphasis:

> Our higher education establishments need to be concerned with attitudes to the world outside education, and in particular to industry and commerce and to beware of 'anti-business' snobbery. The entrepreneurial spirit is essential for the maintenance and improvement of employment, prosperity and publice services. Higher education should be alert to the hazard of blunting it and should seek opportunities to encourage it. More generally, higher education needs to foster positive attitudes to work.
> Higher education's output of able, skilled and well-motivated graduates is vital to the country's economic performance . . . Although a wide range of courses is available at different levels to meet the needs of industry, commerce, the professions and the public services, there is continuing concern that higher education does not always respond sufficiently to changing economic needs.
> Institutions and academic staff have a responsibility to seek closer links with employers, which are essential if higher education is to realize its full potential in meeting the needs of the economy, in terms of highly qualified manpower and also of its contribution through research, technology transfer and consultancy [. . .] (Green Paper, 1985).

Suggested Remedies

Most of the published works quoted thus far devote much more space to recounting what is wrong than to indicating how matters might be put right. The National Economic Development Council report, however, does go into considerable detail regarding possible remedies. A main obstacle was seen to be the examination system which dominates much of the work of schools and has an 'almost exclusively academic orientation'; in particular the proliferation of the 23 separate GCE and CSE examining boards and their 'effective autonomy from influences outside the education sector' made it difficult to introduce change. Whether the new GCSE (General Certificate of Secondary Education) examination (introduced in 1986/87) to replace both GCE O-level and CSE, will substantially alter the situation in this regard is at present not entirely clear but there are at least grounds for thinking that it will.

If part of the problem lies with the teachers themselves then a share of blame, in the NEDC view, must also be attributed to the training they receive: teacher training courses rarely include more than the briefest of references to employment and the world of work and the combined demands of the training system make entry difficult for persons with desirable industrial experience. Both initial and in-service training needed adaptation directly to reflect the fact that 'the industrial world which pupils face has been and is changing rapidly'. And thirdly, according to NEDC, the system of financing education needed reform so as to gear resources more directly to the remedies needed: an obvious example related to the shortage of well-qualified teachers of mathematics, science and technical subjects where additional resources or financial incentives could be provided. And finally it was up to industry itself to articulate its demands much more clearly, probably through the establishment of an appropriate national body which could speak with one coherent voice for the needs of industry.

These points are not, of course, new; they have all appeared elsewhere on previous occasions. In the 1980s, however, it does seem that they are being put forward with a new emphasis and urgency. In the general field of links between education and industry several new initiatives have taken place in recent years, mainly on the lines of giving the education curriculum a greater vocational orientation. Both the educational system and industrial organizations have tried to respond to the various criticisms that have been expressed. The most significant of the new moves have been the Certificate of Pre-Vocational Education (CPVE) and Technical and Vocational Education Initiative (TVEI) courses.

Notes

1. White Paper (1985) *Better Schools* (Cmnd 9469), DES/HMSO.
2. Green Paper (1985) *The Development of Higher Education into the 1990s* (Cmnd 9524), DES/HMSO.
3. Crowther Report (1959) *15 to 18*, Report of the Central Advisory Council for Education (England), HMSO.
4. Newsom Report (1963) *Half Our Future*, Report of the Central Advisory Council for Education (England), HMSO.
5. Robbins Report (1963) *Higher Education* (Cmnd 2154) HMSO.
6. Dainton Report (1968) *Enquiry into the Flow of Candidates in Science and Technology into Higher Education* (Cmnd 3541), HMSO.
7. Russell Report (1973) *Adult Education: A Plan for Development*, HMSO.
8. Carter, M. (1966) *Into Work*, Pelican.
9. *The Times Educational Supplement* (1976) 22 October.
10. Green Paper (1977) *Education in Schools* (Cmnd 6869), HMSO.

3

The Growth of Central Influence on the Curriculum

GORDON KIRK*

The Historical Context

Who should determine what young people learn at school? That has been a keenly disputed question in Britain for more than a hundred years. As public education developed in the middle of the nineteenth century, and as public funds were allocated for this purpose, it was considered that central government should oversee what was taught in schools. If investment in public education was a necessary political and humanitarian response to the problems of poverty and underprivilege, if it was an appropriate means of fostering and maintaining religious adherence, and if it was calculated to equip young people with the skills demanded by a changing industrial society, then a strategy had to be found for ensuring that value was obtained for the funds invested. According to the Newcastle Commission of 1861, the best means of obtaining that assurance was

> to institute a searching examination by a competent authority of every child in every school to which grants are to be paid with the view of ascertaining whether these indispensable elements of knowledge are thoroughly acquired and to make the prospects and position of the teacher dependent, to a considerable extent, on the results of this examination.[1]

In 1862 the Revised Code instituted a system of grants for schools: 8s (40p) per year was to be awarded for every pupil who attended more than 200 times. Moreover, all pupils were to be subject to annual tests in reading, writing and arithmetic, administered by HMI, and 2s. 8d. (approximately 14p) was to be deducted from the grant for each test a child failed. Such were the main features of the strategy known as 'payment by results'. Through that strategy the machinery of the state was deployed to control the work of teachers, to prescribe standards of achievement in a narrow range of

*Source: From Cosin, B., Flude, M., and Hales, M. (eds.) (1989) *School Work and Equality : A Reader*, Hodder & Stoughton, London.

objectives. Representatives of the central government were required to judge whether or not these standards had been achieved.

The system of payment by results was abolished in 1895. Nevertheless central control of the elementary school curriculum was maintained through a succession of codes and it was not until 1936 that these regulations were changed in a way that left responsibility for 'a suitable curriculum and syllabus with due regard to the organization and circumstances of the school' in the hands of teachers. Indeed, as far as secondary schools were concerned the stranglehold exerted by central government over the curriculum was not relaxed until the 1944 Education Act for England and Wales and the corresponding Scottish legislation of 1945.

While the system of 'payment by results' was formally abolished in 1895 it has continued over the years to represent an enormous affront to the professional consciousness of teachers and a threat to the creation of an effective educational service. There are three grounds for this pervasive professional opposition to the system. First, 'payment by results' demeaned education and reduced it to a mere cramming exercise in which all that is expected of pupils is a capacity for recall. Secondly, the system circumscribed professional activity, constrained initiative, and demanded acquiescence in a curriculum that was so narrowly conceived as to represent a parody of education. Finally, 'payment by results' has been interpreted to exemplify a state-controlled curriculum, the deliberate use of political power to mould the minds of the young. For these reasons, 'payment by results' has remained anathema to teachers and their professional associations. Consequently, any measure which seeks to strengthen central influence on the curriculum and to weaken teachers' autonomy in curriculum matters is still likely to evince the same suspicion and hostility with which teachers responded to 'payment by results'. This deeply ingrained suspicion of central government explains the aversion of teachers to any increase of ministerial involvement in curricular matters.

In the years between 1862 and 1944/45 there was a significant lessening of central control of the school curriculum; the years since then have witnessed an equally significant shift in the opposite direction. The extent of that shift can be illustrated by two ministerial pronouncements. The first, attributed to George Tomlinson, the Minister of Education from 1947 in the post-war Labour government, intimated with concise frankness that the 'Minister knows nowt about curriculum'. The second, uttered by Sir Keith Joseph, the Conservative Secretary of State for Education and Science in the present government, in a speech at Sheffield in January 1984 was no less frank:

> I can offer an account of what the minimum level to be attained at 16 by 80%–90% of pupils would entail in a few areas of the curriculum . . .; in English, pupil would need to demonstrate that they are attentive listeners and confident speakers when dealing with everyday matters of which they have experience, that they can read straightforward written

information and pass it on—orally and in written form—without loss of meaning and that they can say clearly what their own views are; in Mathematics, that they can apply the topics and skills in the foundation list proposed in the Cockcroft Report; in Science, that they are willing and able to take a practical approach to problems, involving sensible observations and appropriate measurements and can communicate their findings effectively . . .; in History, that they possess some historical knowledge and perspective, understand the concepts of cause and consequence, and can compare and extract information from historical evidence and be aware of its limitations; and in CDT [craft, design and technology], that they can design and make something, using a limited range of materials and calling on a resticted range of concepts and give an account of what they have done and the problems they encountered.[2]

The first statement, evoking a tradition of political non-interference in the curriculum, repudiates the locus of central government from such matters. The second, by contrast, is a striking use of ministerial authority to influence what is taught in the schools and is indicative of the assertive pursuit of government policy to wield such influence. This chapter seeks to chart the growth of that government assertiveness and to highlight some of the significant manifestations of its emergence.

James Callaghan's Ruskin Speech, 1976

There is evidence that, traditionally, ministers in successive governments were persuaded to adopt a neutral stance on the curriculum. One indeed, the Conservative Minister David Eccles, is reputed to have alluded to 'the secret garden of the curriculum'. That metaphor of the curriculum as forbidden territory to ministers was directly challenged by Mr Callaghan's speech at Ruskin College, Oxford, in October 1976. The Prime Minister was clearly motivated by growing public concern about education and the work of the schools. His brief for the speech was prepared by the DES and was leaked to the press in advance. The Yellow Paper, as the leaked document came to be called, was critical of teaching in primary and secondary schools. It claimed that some teachers in the primary school had allowed performance in the basic skills of reading, writing and arithmetic to be adversely affected by their inadequate understanding and hence uncritical application of child-centred, or informal, methods. With regard to the secondary school curriculum, the Yellow Paper maintained that too much scope had been given to the principle of pupil choice, with the result that many pupils were following unbalanced programmes and not enough pupils were studying science-based and technological subjects. The antidote to these ills was thought to lie in the institution of a core or common component in the curriculum of all pupils.

The Prime Minister's speech was eagerly anticipated by the educational and wider community and it duly received the full media treatment. However, if people expected a lucid analysis of the ills of contemporary education, together with appropriate and carefully contrived proposals for change, they were disappointed. The speech had more modest objectives. First, it implicitly and explicitly asserted that the aims of education and the content of the curriculum were legitimate matters for public discussion and could not be looked upon as the exclusive concern of professionals:

> I take it that no one claims exclusive rights in this field. Public interest is strong and legitimate and will be satisfied. . . . Parents, teachers, learned and professional bodies, representatives of higher education and both sides of industry, together with the government, all have an important part to play in formulating and expressing the purpose of education and the standards that we need.[3]

Of course, the very fact that the Prime Minister made the speech at all, and that he had rejected the advice 'to keep off the grass', as he put it, was a powerful reinforcement of the case he was arguing. Secondly, the speech identified issues that, in the Prime Minister's judgement, were the source of public concern and required public debate. Among the issues raised were the following: deficiency in the basic skills among school-leavers; the reluctance of many of our best trained students to join industry; standards of literacy and numeracy; the value of informal teaching methods; the place of 'a basic curriculum with universal standards'; and 'the role of the Inspectorate in relation to national standards'. Very clearly, the Prime Minister saw the speech as an opportunity to set the agenda for an extended public discussion of educational issues. The 'Great Debate' followed.

The Great Debate, 1967–77

The Great Debate took place at two levels. First, it was represented by a massive output of articles in the educational and the national press about standards, about the composition of the core curriculum, about the control of the curriculum, and about the role of the schools and other related matters. Secondly, at a more formal level, it took the form of eight regional one-day conferences. To each of these there were invited about 200 representatives of the world of industry and commerce, trade unions, teachers' associations, local education authorities and institutions of higher education. The background paper for these meetings, *Educating our Children: Four Subjects for Debate*, was prepared by the DES. This derived clearly from the issues raised in the Prime Minister's Ruskin speech. The four subjects for debate were:

(1) The school curriculum 5–16.
(2) The assessment of standards.
(3) The education and training of teachers.
(4) School and working life.

Among the issues for discussion of the first two subjects were the following:

(1) What should be the aims and content of a core curriculum?
(2) How best can an agreed core curriculum be put into effect?
(3) Do we have adequate means of obtaining reliable information about the performance of pupils in schools and, if not, what further measures are required?

What value was served by these regional conferences? According to one commentator, the format allowed little more than 'a short canter for a stable of hobby horses'.[4] Another verdict was that the Great Debate was 'a unique exercise in contemplating the country's educational navel'.[5] For her part, the Minister, Shirley Williams, expressed satisfaction at this move towards open consultation on the part of the DES. It is not beyond the bounds of possibility that the regional conferences demonstrated such a diversity of views on important aspects of educational policy that the way was left clear for a more decisive lead from the centre. That lead was speedily forthcoming.

Education in Schools: A Consultative Document (The Green Paper), July 1977

The Green Paper from the Department of Education and Science and the Welsh Office demonstrates its relationship to the Ruskin speech and to the issues raised in the Great Debate before moving swiftly to a statement on the partnership between schools, local education authorities and ministers. That statement includes the following justification for central involvement in curriculum matters:

> The Secretaries of State are responsible in law for the promotion of the education of the people of England and Wales. They need to know what is being done by the local education authorities and, through them, what is happening in the schools. They must draw attention to national needs if they believe the educational system is not adequately meeting them.

Then, after alluding to current criticisms of the curriculum, and having asserted the need 'to establish generally accepted principles for the composition of the school curriculum for all pupils', the paper continues:

> It would not be compatible with the duty of the Secretaries of State to 'promote the education of the people of England and Wales', or with their accountability to Parliament, to abdicate from leadership on educational issues which have become a matter of lively public concern. The Secretaries of State will therefore seek to establish a broad agreement with their partners in the educational service on a framework for the curriculum, and in particular on whether, because there are aims common to all schools and to all pupils at certain stages, there should be a 'core' or 'protected' part.

In execution of that policy it was proposed that a circular would be issued to all local authorities asking them to carry out a review of the curriculum in their areas in consultation with their schools and to report the results within about twelve months.

Enquiry into Local Education Authority Arrangements for the Management of the Curriculum

Circular 14.27 was a wide-ranging questionnaire to LEAs covering all aspects of the planning, development, evaluation and resourcing of the curriculum in their schools. Some of the relevant questions were as follows:

- What procedures have the authority established to enable them to carry out their curricular responsibilities under Section 23 of the Education Act (1944)?
- What systematic arrangements, if any, have the authority established for the collection of information about the curricula offered by schools in their area?
- How does the authority help schools decide on the relative emphasis they should give to particulr aspects of the curriculum, especially the promotion of literacy and numeracy?
- What contribution has the authority made to the consideration of the problems faced by secondary schools, of providing suitable subject options for older pupils while avoiding the premature dropping of curricular elements regarded as essential for all pupils?
- What curricular elements does the authority regard as essential?

The replies to the circular were reported in 1979. Two significant findings emerged in relation to the questions quoted above. First, 'most authorities do not have systematic arrangements for regularly collecting and monitoring curricular information from their schools'. Secondly, there was very considerable diversity of view as to what the 'essential elements' of the curriculum should be, many authorities regarding such matters as being the concern of the schools themselves. Given the prevailing views about where responsibility for curricula rested, these findings are not perhaps totally unpredictable. Indeed, one critic of the exercise considered that 'the circular was a device which managed to make LEAs look as if they were failing in their duties, and thus allowed the DES to take the initiative'.[6] For their part, the ministers concerned made their intentions clear. They proposed 'to give a lead in the process of reaching a national consensus on a desirable framework for the curriculum'. Such an initiative would 'give central government a firmer basis for the development of national policies and the deployment of resources; and provide a checklist for authorities and schools in formulating and reviewing their curricular aims and policies in the light of local needs and circumstances. . . . Conceived in this way, an agreed framework could offer a significant step forward in the quest for improvement in the consistency and quality of school education across the country'.[7] As a first step in the development of such a framework, HMI would be invited to formulate 'a view of a possible curriculum on the basis of their knowledge of schools'.

Papers from HM Inspectorate

The writings of HM Inspectorate can be seen to reinforce the commitment to a national framework for the curriculum. In 1977 they produced *Curriculum 11–16*. The first section of that document set out a powerful 'case for a common curriculum in secondary education to 16'. Such a common curriculum was thought to derive from eight 'areas of experience':

(1) the aesthetic and creative;
(2) the ethical;
(3) the linguistic;
(4) the mathematical;
(5) the physical;
(6) the scientific;
(7) the social and political;
(8) the spiritual.

The Inspectorate maintained their attack on the 'unacceptable variety' of curricular provision in their *Aspects of Secondary Education* (1979) and again in *A View of The Curriculum* (1980). The latter document re-emphasized the need for a national curriculum framework and for the delineation of a common core of learning for all pupils. The composition of that core was put forward, rather tentatively, as a series of 'propositions for consideration'. In effect, the inspectorate proposed a core that consisted of English, mathematics, religious education, physical education, modern languages, 'arts and applied crafts', history, and science subjects. Finally, in *The Curriculum from 5 to 16* (1985) the Inspectorate insisted that throughout the period of compulsory schooling all pupils should maintain contact with nine areas of learning—the 1977 list, except that 'technological' learning is added and 'the social and political' is replaced by 'human and social'. In each of these areas of learning schools were urged to cultivate appropriate knowledge, concepts, skills and attitudes, thus ensuring that all pupils received a broadly comparable educational experience.

The National Curriculum Framework

The government made its first attempt at formulating a national curriculum framework in the consultative document *A Framework for the School Curriculum* (1980). In a somewhat terse paper—it being considered that the more substantial analysis of principles had been carried out in the HMI document *A View of the Curriculum*—it was maintained that throughout the period of compulsory schooling, from 5–16, all pupils should undertake study in English, mathematics, science, religious education, and physical education. At the secondary level, the report continued, pupils should study in addition a modern language and the curriculum of all pupils should include what is called 'preparation for adult and working life', a varied programme of activities incorporating craft, design and technology, history and geography, moral education, health education, and 'preparation for parenthood and for a participatory role in adult society'.

The government's thinking was further developed in *The School Curriculum* (1981), which was clearly seen as the culminating point of several years of public discussion. Having reasserted the need for a national framework and having listed a set of general educational aims, the ministers set out 'the approach to the curriculum which they consider should now be followed in the years ahead'. As far as the primary phase of schooling was concerned, the plan of development favoured the same activities as were listed in *A Framework for the School Curriculum*, except that more attention was devoted to history and geography, to expressive arts, and to science, and to the need for clearly structured and progressively demanding work in these areas of the curriculum. The framework for the secondary school curriculum was taken to comprise English, mathematics, science, modern languages, microelectronics, craft, design and technology, religious education, physical education, humanities, practical and aesthetic activities, and 'preparation for adult life'.

The paper was seen as constituting 'guidance for local education authorities' and the ministers proposed to inform themselves in due course about the action taken by LEAs with regard to that guidance. That was reinforced in a subsequent circular to LEAs later in 1981 and two years later Circular 8/83 sought a progress report from LEAs on the formation of a curriculum policy for pupils of all abilities and aptitudes.

While *The School Curriculum* might have been seen as the government's definitive statement on the structure of the national curriculum framework, it was superseded in September 1984 by *The Organization and Content of the 5–16 Curriculum*, although the wording of the latest document conveyed the impression that the final nature and scope of the national framework has not yet been determined. The structure of the curriculum proposed for the primary phase is similar to that set out in earlier documentation but includes the following additional components:

- craft and practical work leading to some experience of design and technology and of solving problems;
- introduction to computers;
- insights into the adult world, including how people earn their living.

The proposed structure for the secondary phase is similar to that in *The School Curriculum* except that specific provision is made in the latest document for Home Economics for all pupils.

There is one feature of these developments that is worth highlighting. Throughout the official documents there is a disclaimer about the government's intention. Repeatedly it is urged that there is no intention to introduce, through legislation, a nationally prescribed curriculum that would be binding on all LEAs and on all schools. Thus, *Curriculum 11–16* (1977) from HMI avers:

We repeat that it is not the intention to advocate a standard curriculum for all secondary schools to the age of 16, not least because that would be educationally naive. One of the greatest assets of our educational arrangements is the freedom of schools to respond to differing circumstances in their localities and to encourage the enterprise and strength of their teachers.

Indeed, the government's own document, *The School Curriculum* (1981) includes these words: 'Neither the government nor the local authorities should specify in detail what the schools should teach.' At the same time, there is evidence that the government's interest in the school curriculum was not limited to the institution of a national framework. The White Paper, *Better Schools* (1985), indicated that one of the government's major policy commitments was 'to secure greater clarity about the objectives and content of the curriculum', that being considered a necessary step towards the improvement of standards achieved by pupils. That policy is being pursued in two ways: first, the DES is publishing a series of documents on the objectives to be sought in the different areas of the curriculum. To date, the documentation has appeared on English (DES, 1984)[8] and Science (DES, 1985).[9] Both documents seek to identify the skills and understandings which their respective subjects should seek to achieve at different stages of schooling. Secondly, ministers have approved 'national criteria' for different subject areas. These national criteria have been designed in connection with the new General Certificate of Secondary Education and are intended to 'offer a concise account of the understanding, knowledge and competences which should be developed in the course of following the syllabus'. Without question, these developments will impose very powerful constraints on the schools and mark a decisive shift of power in curricular matters to the centre. It is not surprising that a leading official of the NUT should dismiss the White Paper which collates the present government's curricular initiatives as 'a dose of centralist rhetoric'.[10]

For its part, the government insists that 'the establishment of broadly agreed objectives would not mean that the curricular policies of the Secretary of State, the LEA and the school should relate to each other in a nationally uniform way. In the government's view, such diversity is healthy, accords well with the English and Welsh traditions of school education and makes for liveliness and innovation.'[11]

Arguably, what has occurred is a reinterpretation of the traditional partnership between central government, LEAs and schools which has allowed central government, on the basis of its 'accountability to parliament for the performance of the educational service at all levels', progressively to nudge LEAs into a fuller appreciation of their curricular responsibilities and, through that, to influence the schools. The strategy consisted not of ministerial *diktat* but the progressive application of pressure on LEAs to ensure that the school curriculum in their areas was in line with a real or imagined consensus about what pupils should learn at school. At the same time, there were other events which very considerably strengthened the lead from the centre and made it more likely that LEAs would respond positively to the government's initiatives. These are considered in the remainder of this chapter.

The Demise of the Schools Council

The Schools Council (for curriculum and examinations), was established in 1964 by the Secretary of State for Education and Science as an independent body with the function of 'the promotion of education by carrying out research into, and keeping under review, curricula, teaching methods and examinations in schools'. It was funded jointly by the DES and LEAs and its membership was deliberately designed to achieve a majority of teachers. Over the years, the Schools Council was responsible for a prodigious output of reports and materials on every aspect of the school curriculum. It very definitely constituted the most significant and influential curriculum development agency in the country and many of its projects attracted international acclaim.

In keeping with its standing as an independent body with a built-in majority of teachers, the Council was committed to the thesis that 'each school should have the fullest measure of responsibility for its own curriculum and teaching methods based on the needs of its own pupils and evolved by its own staff'. It saw its function not to produce curricular prescriptions but rather 'to extend the range of possibilities open to teachers, and to provide them with the most detailed research evidence on which their judgement can be exercised'.[12] Indeed, even when the Schools Council diverted its attention to the whole curriculum, in contrast to its preoccupation with individual areas or aspects, it maintained its non-recommendatory stance. *The Whole Curriculum* (1975) and *The Practical Curriculum* (1981) both sought to alert teachers to the complex issues that have to be taken into account in whole curriculum planning, but both eschewed the provision of ready-made answers. The Schools Council could therefore be seen as testifying vigorously to two principles—curriculum diversity and teacher control of the curriculum.

Over the years, the relationship between the DES and the Schools Council was characterized by what one commentator has described as 'captiousness'. The confidential Yellow Paper, indeed, dismissed the achievements of the Council as 'generally mediocre'. Reservations continued to be expressed about the power of teacher unions in the Council and there were those who felt that 'the curriculum was too important to be left to teachers'. In October 1981, the government's review of the Schools Council, conducted by Nancy Trenaman, concluded that, although the Council had been 'too political, too complicated and was over-stretched', it should nevertheless continue in existence, albeit in a slimmer form. Notwithstanding that report, conducted on behalf of the government, Sir Keith Joseph intimated in April 1982 that he proposed to terminate the Schools Council and to institute two new bodies—the School Curriculum Development Committee and the Secondary Examinations Council—to carry out certain advisory functions relating to the curriculum on the one hand and examinations on the other. Sir Keith made it clear that the membership of the two new committees would comprise 'persons nominated by the Secretary of State for their fitness for this particular important responsibility'. That was the ministerial response to Nancy Trenaman's claim that a nominated body is consistent . . . with a system of central government control of curriculum and examinations'. In the Commons debate which followed the ministerial announcement, there were some MPs who welcomed the demise of 'a nonsensical curriculum development body that has done nothing but damage education over the years'. Others, however, objected to the replacement of the Schools Council by two unelected bodies; they saw dangers in the minister 'surrounding himself by people of one opinion', and in the 'centralized patronage' which was said to characterize the new arrangements, and they detected the eclipse of the values of curriculum pluralism for which the Schools Council had stood.[13] Indeed, one commentator has maintained that the very success of the Schools Council may have hastened its downfall. 'It is ironic that the Council's projects, most of them in one way or another emphasizing the value of local initiative, teacher involvement, school-level decision-making and various innovations in pedagogy such as inter-disciplinary teaching, should lead to heightened activity nationally to control the curriculum'.[14]

The Rise of the Assessment of Performance Unit (APU)

The APU was instituted by the DES in 1974 'to promote the development of methods of assessing and monitoring the achievements of children at school, and to seek to identify the incidence of under-achievement'. While the birth of the new unit was intimated in a document dealing with educational disadvantage and the educational needs of immigrants, the work of the unit has very clearly been concerned with the more general question of standards of achievement in schools. The proponents of the APU insisted that government is bound to maintain an interest in the quality of education in order to determine whether resources are being rationally deployed and whether the schools are serving the changing needs of pupils and of society. To that end, ways had to be found of monitoring the achievements of pupils.

The initial strategy planned by APU was to examine pupils' performances not in the recognized school subjects but in certain areas of development— the verbal, mathematical, scientific, ethical (subsequently changed to social and personal), aesthetic and physical. To date, surveys of achievement have been undertaken in language (with separate provision for foreign languages), mathematics, and science, but not in the three remaining areas.

Jean Dawson, administrative head of APU, summarizes the achievements of the unit in these words:

We have now carried out successfully a total of 27 national surveys without undue disruption to schools, with the general support of the LEAs and teachers concerned . . . and with the enthusiastic co-operation of the children we have tested. . . . Many of the suspicions which existed when the unit was set up, both about the political motivation for its creation and the likely effects of national monitoring on the curriculum, have been allayed (if not entirely put to rest) by the way in which the exercise has been carried out, by the sensitivities displayed by the monitoring teams, by the way in which groups of teachers up and down the country have been involved in the development, trialling and pre-testing of material, and by the cool, impartial way in which the results have been presented.[15]

At the same time there were others who were resolutely opposed to the APU and its philosphy. They doubted whether valid measures of *all* of the areas of development could be devised; they maintained that the tests used would have a distorting and trivializing effect on pupils' learning ('this year's test becomes next year's curriculum'): they pointed to the possibility, notwithstanding the assurances that light sampling techniques would be deployed, that superficial comparisons would be made on the basis of inadequate evidence between areas and between schools; and they detected in the paraphernalia of mass testing associated with the APU the most sinister intrusion of central government into the work of the schools and the spectre of state-controlled curricula.

The Reform of the Examination System at 16 +

It is widely acknowledged that the school examination system has exerted a powerful controlling effect on school curricula, even if, in more recent times, CSE (Mode 3) has allowed schools to play a significant role on the assessment of their own pupils. While, for many years, there has been discussion, in the Schools Council and elsewhere, about the reform of the examination system and the closer integration of CSE and GCE, Sir Keith Joseph gave notice in January 1984 of much more radical changes in the assessment of pupils at the end of compulsory schooling. He envisaged a shift, in line with modern educational thinking, away from a system in which pupils are assessed in relation to each other (a norm-referenced system) to one in which they would be assessed in relation to certain pre-specified criteria (a criterion-referenced system). In the latter, pupils succeed or 'pass' if they reach certain levels of competence: they are expected to give evidence of having reached a particular level of performance regardless of how they stand in relation to their peers. These features will characterize the new General Certificate of Secondary Education in England and Wales.

Sir Keith Joseph has intimated that 'national' criteria will be established in the main curriculum areas. This development will call for detailed research in order to establish clearly and unambiguously the skills and understandings testified by a given level of achievement. In this way, a system is expected to evolve in which teachers, employers, further and higher education, as well as pupils, can have confidence in what a given award actually means: it will indicate, clearly, what a pupil has been able to achieve. Whether or not a reform of this kind will lead, as Sir Keith Joseph maintained, to a general raising of standards of achievement, it has been interpreted as a further encroachment on the part of central government into what is taught and learned in schools. Indeed, if performance criteria are to be *national*, if they are to have currency throughout the system, and if they are to be as detailed and specific as the proponents of criterion-referenced testing insist, then this reform presages central intervention in the school curriculum of a most emphatic kind.

Government Policy on Standards

As has been noted, signs of a more active interest of central government in the school curriculum were apparent under the Labour administration in the 1970s. It is arguable that this interest has intensified under the present Conservative government. That government made standards in education a principal plank in its election platform and the action undertaken by that government in relation to curriculum and assessment is part of a wider and coherent strategy on standards in education. That strategy incorporates a review of the content of courses of initial teacher training; the establishment of a committee for the accreditation of courses of teacher education; an inquiry into the procedures for the external validation of courses in public sector higher education; an inquiry into selection for teaching; suggestions for regular staff appraisal of teachers, and the public reporting by Her Majesty's Inspectorate of their findings on visits to schools and colleges.

Technical and Vocational Education Initiative (TVEI)[16]

In November 1982 the Prime Minister announced the government's intention to launch TVEI, a five-year project to be conducted by the Manpower Services Commission 'to explore and test methods of organizing, managing and resourcing replicable programmes of general, technical and vocational education for young people between the ages of 14 and 18'. This initiative was designed to stimulate local authorities to mount full-time programmes which would be funded from central funds—to the extent of £400,000 per project—provided that they met certain centrally determined criteria relating to equal opportunities, progression, the specification of objectives, the balance between general, technical and vocational elements of programmes, planned work experience, and assessment. Projects in Scotland had, in addition, to demonstrate their compatibility with national curriculum development initiatives for 14–16-year-olds and 16–18-year-olds.

In the first year of its operation TVEI sponsored fourteen projects; in its second year a further 48 projects were mounted, including five in Scotland. In 1985 a further eleven programmes were introduced in England and Wales and one more in Scotland.

While the Schemes are voluntary, in the sense that LEAs are not obliged to mount them and pupils are not compulsorily involved, and while the programmes demonstrate the variety that is to be expected from vigorous local initiatives, the significance of TVEI is unmistakable. As the responsibility of the Department of Employment, TVEI represents a determined government effort, practically by-passing the government department that has traditionally exercised responsibility for the schools and the school curriculum, to effect a swift and decisive orientation of the curriculum towards what is considered to be of immediate relevance to the skills and know-how required by a technological society.

Legislating for the National Curriculum

The discussion so far has sought to trade the progressive involvement of Central Government in the shaping of the school curriculum and to point to certain other government initiatives which undeniably strengthened the centralist trend. All of these developments and initiatives culminated in the government's consultative paper of July 1987 entitled *The National Curriculum 5–16*,[17] which gave notice that the Secretary of State proposed to introduce legislation to establish a national curriculum. The proposed national curriculum contained many familiar ingredients:

Mathematics ⎫
English   ⎬ The Core
Science   ⎭

Modern/Foreign Language (not in primary schools)
Technology
History
Geography
Art
Music
Physical Education

However, the paper went well beyond the delineation of a framework: it proposed the establishment in each subject area of 'attainment targets' for pupils at age 7, 11, 14 and 16, as well as 'programmes of study' setting out 'the overall content, knowledge, skills and processes relevant to today's needs which pupils should be taught'. Furthermore, 'nationally prescribed tests' would be administered at each of the age levels mentioned to determine the extent to which the prescribed targets have been achieved. Finally, the bodies created by Sir Keith Joseph—the School Curriculum

Development Committee and the Secondary Examination Council—would be replaced by a National Curriculum Council and a School Examinations and Assessment Council, both appointed by the Secretary of State, with responsibility to offer him advice on the national curriculum and its assessment. These proposals, virtually unchanged as a result of the consultation process, were embodied in the Education Reform Bill placed before parliament in November 1987.

While these features of the proposed legislation were foreshadowed in earlier government papers and initiatives it is worth exploring why it was decided to break from the practice of national consensus seeking through discussion and persuasion and to introduce legislation. There are four sets of consideration that are relevant in this connection.

In the first place, the Conservative government had just been re-elected, in June 1987, with a substantial majority. The opportunity afforded by a third term in office is thought to have induced a 'triumphalist' determination to effect even more remarkable and radical transformations in the social order than were brought about since it first took office in 1979. And what more radical initiative in education could be mounted than one which decisively disturbed the traditional partnership between central and local government in the management of education and which exploded once and for all the myth of 'the secret garden of the curriculum'?

A second set of factors justifying legislation are adduced in the consultation paper itself. There it is maintained that, despite a decade of public discussion on the curriculum and the existence of widespread agreement on its main features, there were significant variations in practice which needed to be eliminated in the interests of equipping all young people 'with the knowledge, skills and understandings that they need for adult life and employment'. Legislation clearly was seen as the only way to bring about that objective quickly. It was also seen as a way of raising standards of attainment: the specification of targets and the systematic assessment of pupils' work on a national basis were thought to constitute a challenge to schools and teachers to raise their expectations, and to channel their efforts to bring about enhanced standards in pupils in the key areas represented by the national curriculum. In this way, individual schools and their teachers would be made more closely accountable for the education they provide since their work will be directly assessable against the results of other schools in the locality and against the national standards. These developments reflect the government's acceptance of the importance of education as the key instrument in the liberation of human talent and as the principal agent of the country's economic regeneration. Since education was such a critical service it was a responsibility of government to determine its content and to ensure that it was effective.

The third feature that needs to be considered in contextualizing the national curriculum legislation is the government's attitude towards local authorities. While the legislation is clearly to be seen as evidence of a government's entitlement to legislate in connection with a national responsibility, it is also interpretable as evidence of the government's impatience with local authorities. There had been a decade of consultation and as recently as 1986 an Education Act had required local authorities to devise policy documentation in relation to the curriculum and its delivery. Even that strategy, however, had still left too much responsibility with authorities. The legislation reflected a judgement that local authorities could not deliver what the national interest required.

It is possible to see the national curriculum legislation as part of the government's strategy to reduce the power of local authorities. Indeed, the years since 1979 have witnessed a continuing struggle between local and national government. While that struggle tended to centre on financial matters—the government's commitment to effect reductions in public expenditure in opposition to local authority commitment to the enhancement of public services—what was at issue was the power of local authorities in relation to the power of central government. Significantly, the Education Reform Bill contains two measures that will curtail local authority powers still further. The first of these will require local authorities to delegate to governing bodies of schools very considerable responsibility for financial management and the appointment of staff. The second allows schools to 'opt out' of local authority control altogether and to be funded directly by central government. At first sight these measures appear to be interestingly decentralist in the sense that they devolve power and responsibility to the local level. In that sense they might be seen to be moving in a different direction from the strongly centralist initiatives in connection with the national curriculum. However, these various measures are perfectly consistent in the sense that they encroach decisively on areas on which local authorities exercise responsibility and, since the Secretary of State will have a key role in connection with financial delegation and 'opting out', the measures must be said to reinforce the centralism which is reflected most obviously in the measures to the national curriculum.

Finally, it is necessary to see the national curriculum legislation in relation to the teaching profession. For two years prior to 1987 there was unprecedented industrial action by teachers which seriously dislocated the educational service. That dispute, which concerned, among other things, teachers' pay and conditions of service, was sustained partly because teachers could exploit contractual arrangements which were imprecise. There have been three government initiatives which were designed to obviate any similar disruption in the future. The Secretary of State has made regulations specifying teachers' contractual obligations in a comprehensive list of duties; he has decided to scrap the long-established machinery in which teachers' pay and conditions were negotiated and has assumed temporary powers to determine these himself; and he has introduced a national curriculum. The last of these, with its prespecified targets, its programmes of study, and its national testing will exercise a powerful constraint on teachers' work. While the consultation paper claims that 'the legislation should leave full scope for professional judgement' and while it insists that the law will provide a framework, 'not a strait-jacket', there are many who will see the legislation as the culmination of a strategy intended to whip teachers into line.

Developments in Scotland

Scotland is a compact educational entity with long experience of strongly centralized modes of operation. The effectiveness of these centralized procedures is demonstrated in the management of the major programme of changes in curriculum and assessment currently taking place in Scotland.

Two national committees were established in 1974, one by the Consultative Committee on the curriculum, the nominated body responsible for advising the Secretary of State on curriculum matters, to examine the structure of the curriculum for 14–16-year-olds (the Munn Committee) and the other by the Secretary of State himself to consider assessment at 16 + (the Dunning Committee). Both committees reported in 1977. Munn advocated a core plus options curriculum pattern, which required pupils to undertake work in each of eight 'modes of activity' as follows:

- linguistic/literary;
- mathematics;
- social studies;
- scientific;
- religious education;
- moral education;
- aesthetic studies;
- physical education.

Dunning recommended a complex pattern of 'assessment for all', covering the whole age range and enabling pupils to reach one of three levels of achievement—merit, general or foundation—in each area of study. Following extensive feasibility studies into timetabling arrangements and the technical aspects of the assessment proposals, the Secretary of State produced his response to the reports in 1980 in the shape of a circular from SED (No. 10/93) which included these words:

> All schools are asked to adopt the curriculum framework provided by the eight modes of study provided by the Munn Committee. Within that framework schools and education authorities are in the best position to judge the particular form which the curriculum should take in the light of each school's individual circumstances and the needs of its pupils. Nevertheless, there are certain overriding priorities and the Secretary of State considers that it is essential that all pupils in the third and fourth years of secondary education should study English, Mathematics and Science.

Thus a national curriculum framework was introduced without recourse to legislation: the Secretary of State merely exercised a traditional entitlement to influence. The Secretary of State's authority on this matter has been accepted, not out of docility or in the belief that the Secretary of State for Scotland is infallible in curriculum matters: it has been accepted because it is very obviously based on a clear national consensus. That consensus was reflected in the recommendations of the Munn Committee itself, which were, in turn, based on the evidence submitted to the committee. It was also reflected in the public discussion that took place following the publication of the report. Without probing too deeply into the reasons for the emergence of that national consensus—and the cogency of the Munn report's argument and the compactness of Scotland as an educational entity, cannot be disregarded in this connection—the existence of that consensus is beyond question and it undoubtedly made the introduction of a national curriculum framework a relatively unproblematic matter. The Secretary of State's announcement reflected what, in the light of the consultation and public discussion, local authorities and schools wished to see.

When the Secretary of State endorsed the curriculum framework proposed by Munn he also intimated that the assessment proposals foreshadowed in the Dunning report would be implemented. After further piloting of appropriate curriculum and assessment materials the Secretary of State intimated in 1982 that there would be a phased implementation of the proposals, beginning in August 1984. That decision called for the establishment of joint working parties, for each of the subject areas, with responsibility for devising guidelines for the new syllabus and specifying the detailed criteria relating to their assessment. The activities of these joint working parties was extensive and entailed the substantial involvement of teachers in Scotland in curriculum development work. The intention clearly was to make sure that guidelines developed reflected enterprising classroom practice. Besides, within the central guidelines, schools and teachers themselves were expected to exercise their skills and responsibilities for determining what pupils should learn.

Unfortunately for the government's programme, for most of 1985 and 1986, Scottish teachers conducted a massive programme of industrial action which seriously disrupted the work of the schools. Besides, since the industrial action involved a boycott of curriculum development, the carefully planned implementation of Standard Grade, as the reforms came to be known, was completely undermined. Scottish teachers, like their counterparts south of the border, were seeking better pay and conditions; but the Scottish dispute was also a massive protest at the rapid rate of educational change and at the way in which teachers felt they were expected to carry forward developments without adequate support. The longer the dispute continued the more officialdom in Scottish education recognized that support had to be provided. That took two forms. In the first place, a working party set up to simplify the complex technicalities of the original assessment proposals generated a system which was more intelligible and rational. Secondly, before the dispute ended, for each major area of the curriculum there was established a central support group with responsibility for developing exemplar and other materials relating to the Standard Grade programme. Some of these central support groups worked in collaboration with local support groups of teachers and others in an effort to ensure that the centrally endorsed materials were rooted in classroom experience.

The agreement which marked the end of the dispute late in 1986 concluded that, since the preparation of teaching materials to support curriculum development had been a major burden on individual teachers, henceforth curriculum development should be supported by exemplars and other teacher materials prepared by secondees and voluntary working groups. It is difficult not to see in that agreement what has come to be called the 'cascade' model of curriculum development: materials are prepared centrally and passed down the line for the classroom functionaries to implement. One critic has described the model as 'an unholy alliance of enthusiasts for strong management with a sufficient number of apathetic teachers'.[18]

There are two other developments in Scotland that require to be highlighted. The first concerns the government's 16+ Action Plan. Envisaged as a comprehensive restructuring of educational provision in further education colleges into 40-hour modules, it is rapidly finding its way into the work of the secondary school. What is noteworthy in the present context is that it was an initiative that was energetically directed by SED and it involved the preparation centrally of curriculum materials for every area of work.

The second development represents an even more emphatic instance of the growth of government influence on the curriculum in Scotland. In November 1987 the government produced a consultation paper entitled *Curriculum and Assessment in Scotland: a policy for the 90s.*[19] The paper proposed for each area of the curriculum for pupils 5–14 'a nationally agreed set of guidelines setting out the aims of study, the content to be covered, and the objectives to be achieved'. In addition, there will be national testing of pupils at age 8 and age 12 in language and mathematics. If required, legislation will be invoked to give effect to the changes.

The appearance of the Scottish document at the same time as the appearance of the national curriculum legislation in England and Wales can be interpreted as evidence of the government's determination to bring the educational system of Scotland into close alignment with that of England and Wales and to exercise strong control over what that educational system is expected to deliver.

Conclusion

The developments traced here demonstrate very clearly a significant shift in the control of the school curriculum both north and south of the border: whereas responsibility for the nature and structure of the curriculum once rested with local authorities and individual schools it will now rest with central government. Moreover, that control, in England and Wales at least, will be reinforced by legislation.

What is remarkable is that this heavily interventionist stance was developed by a government committed 'to rolling back the frontiers of the state' and to the values of consumerism—'parents know best'. Indeed, the reform bill which marks the full extent of government control has been heralded by the Minister, Kenneth Baker, as a parents' charter, maximizing parental choice in education. Apparently, parents know what is best for their children, but not as much as the Minister!

While the balance of power has decisively shifted, it is worth considering some of the educational implications of the transformation this chapter has attempted to describe. Throughout the period under discussion, successive government initiatives stimulated vigorous public and professional debate, since even the early tentative moves were treated with the suspicion that they presaged even more decisive government 'interference' in what was a local or professional matter. Reviewing a very protracted and at times heated public discussion it is possible to identify three major concerns. It is necessary to consider these in relation to the legislative position in England and Wales and the *de facto* position in Scotland.

The first of these has its roots in the pupil-centred view of education. While this view has various formulations its central stance is that *the purpose of education is to enable pupils to develop with deeper insight and sophistication activities which *they* value or find interesting in ways and contexts which *they* find amenable. On this view, educational systems need to make maximum provision for pupil choice, for curriculum negotiation, and for pupils themselves to determine the lines of their own educational development. Government control or determination of the curriculum, it has been claimed, is a threat to pupil-centred education of this kind. At best, it could kill interest in learning: at worst it could foster the alienation of the young.

The second concern relates to the impact of a government-controlled curriculum on social pluralism. Many see life in the modern context as being characterized by wide diversity. Ours is thought to be a multi-faith, multi-ethnic and multi-cultural society, one in which diversity of life-style flourishes and which tolerates and fosters social and individual differences. Schools, on this view, should protect diversity; they should reflect local variety and the features of widely differing neighbourhoods and subcultures. By contrast, the argument runs, a nationally prescribed curriculum, rigidly dispensed to all, will be a force for dull uniformity in which the vitality and diversity of personal and social experience is homogenized.

Thirdly, the move towards a national curriculum was resisted most strongly by those, mainly teachers and other educationalists, who claimed that the nature and scope of the school curriculum was a professional and not a political matter. They defended the entitlement of teachers, by virtue of their education and training if not their professional standing, to shape the learning experience of pupils and to devise a curriculum suited to the characteristics of their own pupils. That assertion of professional autonomy was thought to be reinforced by studies which stressed that curriculum development should be school-based, rooted in the professional context of teachers rather than in distant centres such as Whitehall or Edinburgh. Teachers, it was felt, were the guardians of a politically free curriculum: if they lost their entitlement to control the learning experiences of pupils, not only would their own professionalism be undermined, but, worse, schools could easily become the agents for transmitting 'state-approved knowledge'.

How have these concerns been affected by the government's assumption of control in curriculum matters? Arguably, the concerns highlighted could be allayed if the government initiatives were concerned with the establishment of a national curriculum framework only. Thus, it is conceivable that, within such a framework, pupils could enjoy considerable opportunities for choice, for curriculum negotiation and for pupil-centred learning. It is equally possible that within such a framework schools and communities could offer curricula that reflected the responsiveness and diversity that many value. Finally, if teachers were left to enjoy full responsibility for the specific content and teaching strategies to be deployed within each of the major categories of the national curriculum framework, there would be no infringement of teachers' professional autonomy and the curriculum could be protected from unjustified political interference. That is to say, a national curriculum framework is logically not incompatible with pupil-centred learning, with the protection of cultural diversity, and with the professional autonomy of teachers. However, it is clear that ministerial control will extend well beyond the determination of a national curriculum framework. On both sides of the border there is a clear government commitment to the development of curriculum guidelines, and the specification of curriculum objectives and content in each subject area, all of which will require the approval of a central government agency. That is to say, the initiatives that are under way, far from alleviating concerns repeatedly expressed over the years, appear to be confirming the worst suspicions of teachers and other commentators. The defenders of the new arrangements will no doubt claim that there is still reasonable scope for pupil-centred learning, for cultural diversity, and for the exercise of professional autonomy, even within a nationally determined curriculum framework. It is too easy to slip into a mood of depression at the outset of what promises to be a period of very significant change in education but, in relation to the concerns identified earlier, it would have to be said that the omens are not propitious.

Notes

1. Lawton, Denis (1980) *The Politics of the School Curriculum*. London: Routledge & Kegan Paul, pp. 15–16.
2. Joseph, Sir Keith (1984) speech to North of England Education Conference, Sheffield, as reported in *Times Educational Supplement*, 13 January.
3. Callaghan, James (1976) Towards a National Debate, speech at Ruskin College, October 1976, as reported in *Education*, 22 October.
4. Quoted in Devlin, Tim and Warnock, Mary (1977) *What must we teach?* London: Temple.
5. Ibid., p. 11.
6. Holt, Maurice (1983) *Curriculum Workshop: An Introduction to Whole Curriculum Planning*. London, Routledge & Kegan Paul, p. 21.
7. DES (Department of Education and Science Welsh Office) (1979) *Local Authority Arrangements for the School Curriculum*, Report on the Circular 14.77 Review. London: HMSO.
8. DES (Department of Education and Science) (1984) *English from 5–16*. London: HMSO.
9. DES (Department of Education and Science) (1985) *Science 5–16: A Statement of Policy*. London: HMSO.
10. *The Sunday Times*, 31 March 1985, p. 17
11. DES (Department of Education and Science) (1985) *Better Schools*. London: HMSO.
12. The Schools Council (1975) Working Paper 53. *The Whole Curriculum 13–16*, London: Evans/Methuen Educational.
13. *Hansard*, 22 April 1982.
14. Skilbeck, Malcolm (1984) Curriculum Evaluation at the National Level, in Skilbeck, Malcolm (ed.), *Evaluating the Curriculum in the Eighties*. London: Hodder & Stoughton.
15. Dawson, Jean (1984), The Work of the Assessment of Performance Unit, in Skilbeck, Malcolm (ed.), *Evaluating the Curriculum in the Eighties*. London: Hodder & Stoughton.
16. *TVEI Review 1984* (1984). London: Manpower Services Commission.
17. DES (Department of Education and Science Welsh Office) (1987) *The National Curriculum 5–16*, a consultation document, July.
18. Smyth, Sydney (1987) An Ending, in *Teaching English*, Vol. 20, No. 3, Autumn.
19. SED (Scottish Education Department) (1987) *Curriculum and Assessment in Scotland: a policy for the 90s*, November.

Part 2

Constructing the Curriculum: Alternative Positions

4

Curriculum Styles and Strategies

GAY HEATHCOTE, RICHARD KEMPA and IOLO ROBERTS*

Introduction

If lessons are to be derived from the experiences of past curriculum development work, it is important that in the first instance the range of conceptions and practices should be unfolded that is embedded in these developments. Thereafter, the conceptions and practices, as they emerge, can be subjected to detailed examination as to their characteristics, their strengths and weaknesses, and their appropriateness for different purposes and under different conditions.

[. . .]

Aims, Goals and Objectives and Associated Curriculum Models

Background Comments

Education is a purposeful activity, and the curriculum is the main means whereby the purposes of education are achieved. Therefore, curriculum developers make determined efforts to communicate their own conceptions of the curriculum intentions associated with their projects. The analysis of a wide range of project materials indicates that these intentions are frequently expressed in one of the following two ways, although a mixture of the two is often prevalent:

(i)   the curriculum developer specifies the learning outcomes, in terms of skills—intellectual and manipulative—and attitudes, which the curriculum seeks to foster and instil in the learner. The degree of precision with which such skills and attitudes are specified and the degree of behaviourism which is associated with such specifications

*Source: From the Further Education Curriculum Review and Development Unit, commissioned by the FEU from the Department of Education, University of Keele, Keele.

does, however, vary considerably. We propose that the terms 'aims', 'goals' and 'objectives' be used to denote statements expressing different degrees of precision and behaviourism.

(ii) the curriculum developer specifies the pedagogical procedures to be adopted by teachers and/or the conditions under which learning is to occur. The establishment of such procedures/conditions may require the teacher to depart from his/her customary pedagogic practices and involve him/her in a substantially new teaching situation in which new teaching styles and role relationships between teacher and taught have to be adopted. The assumption underlying the specification of the instructional procedures/ conditions is that through them certain desirable characteristics on the students' part will result, although these are generally not explicitly identified.

Basic Definitions

The terms 'aims', 'goals' and 'objectives' are widely employed to refer to expressions of educational intention but, unfortunately, no uniformity exists as yet in their use for different types of statement. For the purpose of this analysis, at least, it is desirable to apply a coherent set of terms to characterize expressions of intentionality across a wide variety of different subjects and combinations of subjects. The following definitions and distinctions were adopted:

Curricular Aims

These are seen as generalized statements of intent which may relate to the whole or part of a curriculum. Not infrequently, such statements reflect philosophical or educational beliefs and values. Statements of aims are generally vague and tend to have little operational value (descriptively or prescriptively) in relation to the planning, development and implementation of curricula. They can, however, act as a 'reference' against which the tenability of more specific statements of intent (e.g. curricular goals and objectives) can be appraised.

As has been suggested, statements of curricular intentions are classifiable into those relating to the learner and the educational outcomes expected of him [sic] and those which specify particular instructional conditions to be established by teachers. In accordance with this classification, we may distinguish between *learning aims* (i.e. those which express students' learning outcomes) and *teaching aims* (i.e. those describing pedagogical processes and procedures). To avoid undue confusion in the use of the term aims, we propose that the term be qualified as indicated in the preceding sentence, whenever both types of aim appear and that, without such qualification, the term be used to denote student-related (learning) aims only. This is the practice adopted here.

Our concern here is solely with curricular aims, not the broad aims that are applied to the overall process of education and which have their origin in political and philosophical thought.

Objectives

These are relatively narrow and precise statements of educational outcomes expected of the *student*. They are often couched in terms of the sought-for overt behaviours (abilities, skills and attitudes) and may even include a specification of the level of performance expected of the student. The specification of students' learning outcomes in behavioural terms implies that the students' performance is measurable. The degree of precision with which an objective is stated usually depends on the context in which the objective occurs. In curriculum work, for instance, a subject-based objective (e.g. 'the ability to solve quadratic equations') will be relatively broad in scope and afford some flexibility for teacher mediation and interpretation. In contrast, objectives formulated in the educational technology context (e.g. for programmed learning materials) tend to define learning outcomes in a very specific and often narrow sense. It is, therefore, important to be aware of the differential demands made by the context against which the object is set. However, irrespective of the context, statements of objectives should relate entirely to the learner. For example, the following statement from the Open University course on Technology— Materials Processing, satisfies this requirement:

> (the student) should be able to describe the principle sources of hydrocarbons and the problems inherent in their characterization.

Goals

These occupy an intermediate position between aims and objectives, at least in terms of the preciseness with which the desired educational outcomes are expressed. They are statements which may summarize the outcomes specified either for a course or for a curriculum as a whole. In comparison with objectives, goals express generalized behaviour expected of the learner. Unlike curriculum aims, goals retain an element of operationality in that they usually point to some ability, skill or attitude which, after suitable further definition, may be translated into a series of more precise objectives. According to this definition, the following statement from the Schools Council Integrated Science Project (SCISP), may be classified as a goal:

> the ability to organize and formulate ideas in order to communicate them to others.

The term 'general objectives' has recently been introduced by TEC to refer to statements of educational intent which, in terms of the definitions adopted here can sometimes be described as curriculum goals and in other instances as objectives. We prefer the terminology adopted here because it avoids confusion between different types of objectives, that is, general objectives and specific objectives. For the same reason, we advise against a widening of the meaning of the terms 'goals' and 'objectives' to notions such as 'teaching goals' and 'teaching objectives'. These are invariably aimed at the teacher and usually specify aspects of procedures and conditions to be adopted or provided in the pursuit of teaching. They represent statements of intended teacher activities, and not of students' learning outcomes.

An Analysis of Statements of Intent in Various Projects

The Use and Function of Aims, Goals and Objectives

All the curriculum projects and courses analysed during this study contain some listing of the educational intentions underlying them, although there is a great variation both in the nature of these statements and their degree of specificity. The comparison and classification of these statements is sometimes difficult as different curriculum developers use different terminology and give idiosyncratic meanings to identical terms.

The general tendency is for statements which, in the terms of the definition given, may be classed as aims, to have the function of 'legitimizing' a curriculum. They are used to express the general purposes of a curriculum, rather than its specific intentions. Frequently such aims statements are consonant with more general and global aspirations attributed to the educational process as a whole.

Because of their general and non-operational nature, curriculum aims are normally only of limited value in communicating curriculum intentions to curriculum users. Where they do assume significance, though, is in curricula which embody and make explicit certain values, attitudes or opinions held by the curriculum developer, particularly where these depart from the 'traditional' or established norm. They are, therefore, sometimes used to provoke reactions, stir controversy or stimulate re-thinking about educational values. The Open University course 'Art and Environment', for example, uses statements of aims to make public its course development team's conception of the nature of art and art education and art's perceived relationship with the environment. In so doing, it criticizes previous and current educational practice. This is evident from the following statement of aims, according to which art education should 'enable people to bring to the topic of environment a greater element of imagination and feeling than is usually the case'.

Similarly, the Schools Council Humanities Curriculum Project claims as one of its aims the development in students of 'an understanding of social situations and human acts, and of the controversial value issues which they raise'. This statement contains a value judgement insofar as it is both desirable and appropriate that students (in this case, adolescents) should tackle controversial issues in the classroom.

Three recurrent themes from the basis of many of the statements of aims contained in the various curriculum projects which were analysed:

  (i) promotion of the individual's personal and intellectual growth;
 (ii) meeting the needs of the individual in relation to his societal and physical environment;
(iii) meeting the needs of society itself.

These themes are frequently couched in phrases such as 'self-development', 'self-development in relation to others', 'self-realization', 'preparation for life', 'maturity', 'citizenship', 'autonomy of the individual', 'the future needs of young people', and so on. Desirable though these intentions may be, the phrases themselves unfortunately refer to qualities which are difficult to define with precision. Also, since they are presented at a high level of generality and so lack operationality, they can have only limited value in communicating to the curriculum user the actual intentions of a curriculum.

Statements of curriculum aims are often followed by, or linked to, statements which have the qualities of curricular goals in that they point more precisely than aims to the learning outcomes expected of the student.

Curriculum goals, when stated, appear to serve two principal functions:

  (i) they act as a base from which the curriculum planner can formulate objectives, more specific statements relating to students' learning outcomes. Such objectives often apply to parts or sections of a curriculum, rather than the curriculum as a whole. In this situation, the control over such outcomes remains with the curriculum planner, and the teacher's role is that of an 'agent' who seeks to implement the curriculum planner's specific intentions;
 (ii) curriculum goals may act as a 'staging post' at which the responsibility for their translation into more precise specifications of students' learning outcomes is passed from the curriculum planner to the teacher as curriculum implementer or, in certain instances, to the learner. In this case, goals assume the function of a device whereby the curriculum developer communicates his educational intentions to the teacher who will interpret these intentions in the light of his special situation.

Although these functions are closely connected, they appear as alternatives in curricula, the pre-eminence of one or the other depending on a number of variables such as:

(i) the amount of direction which the curriculum planner wishes to impose on the implementing teacher;

(ii) the extent to which the curriculum emphasizes student autonomy in relation to learning outcomes;

(iii) the ability and previous experience of the students for whom the curriculum is intended;

(iv) the curriculum planner's perception of the constraints imposed and opportunities offered by the subject matter.

These observations can be illustrated by reference to a number of curriculum projects and courses. The Science 5–13 project, for example, specifies 150 statements of objectives which are systematized from 8 goals, all of which arise from a consideration of Piaget's developmental pyschology. A Teachers' Handbook explains the derivation of the objectives to the teacher and gives extensive instructions on the means of realizing them. The only area of decision-making delegated to the teacher lies in the choice of activities whereby the objectives can be achieved. In this sense, the curriculum developer exercises a high degree of control over the implementing teacher, as regards the purpose of the education provided for the learner.

In contrast, Project Technology does not exercise this same degree of control. It specifies a number of curricular goals, but their interpretation and translation into more specific statements of learning outcomes is the responsibility of the teacher. There is in this project a commitment to student-centred learning and much value is placed on student experimentation; but the extent to which these characteristics actually appear in a particular case will depend on the way in which the teacher exercises his autonomy over the further specification of student outcome from the goal-level base. This is, of course, fully in accord with the curriculum planner's intention which is that the teacher should share his responsibility with the student and that learning outcomes should be negotiated between teacher and student, taking into consideration the age, ability and previous experience of the student and the matching complexity of the problem-posing and solving which feature centrally in this project.

The second function of curriculum goals, indicated above, gains in importance when teachers who adopt and implement a curriculum are themselves expected to act as course planners and developers. The Geography 14–18 project makes this expectation and claims that curriculum goals:

(i) provide a broad frame of reference within which discussion about the selection of teaching content, learning experiences, teaching strategies and decisions about assessment can take place;

(ii) serve to direct attention to longer-term aspirations which means that teachers, as curriculum planners have to think hard about exactly what they are trying to achieve;

(iii) make explicit, therefore, the assumptions which underlie the choice of curriculum components, the criteria which teachers use when making decisions about the curriculum and divergent views among groups of teachers which might otherwise have remained hidden.*

Thus, statements of curriculum goals can serve as a planning tool for curricula which, although devised at national level (as in the case of the Geography 14–18 project), seek to involve teachers actively in school (or college)-based curriculum development and adaptation. Goals provide a focus for teacher discussion and allow meaningful development work to be undertaken in the full awareness of organizational constraints, teachers' special interests and expertise, existing facilities and other factors which affect successful curriculum implementation.

Generally, curriculum developers refrain from specifying what, in the terminology adopted here, may be described as objectives, and instead restrict themselves to the statement of broadly based curriculum goals without detailing them further. The assumption would seem to be that teachers are fully capable of translating such broad statements into objectives having a high degree of specificity. In the case of straightforward cognitive learning outcomes, this assumption appears entirely reasonable: levels of knowledge to be acquired and the skills to be learned in particular subject areas are often agreed upon by teachers. Thus, a statement such as 'the student should acquire an understanding of the basic laws of chemistry' may be entirely meaningful to a teacher if a consensus view prevails among chemistry teachers as to what constitutes 'understanding' and about what are the 'basic laws of chemistry' to be taught at a particular level. To itemise each such law might be tedious and lead to an inconveniently long list of curricular objectives.

This argument can readily be extended to other areas of learning and it may be said that often the statement of curricular goals, rather than objectives, suffices in order to convey a picture of curricular intentions to the curriculum user. However, there are instances when no consensus view can be claimed to exist among teachers about how particular broadly-based statements should be interpreted and what knowledge content might be associated with them. For example, the goals of the Schools Council Integrated Science Project state that students should acquire an

> understanding of the significance, including the limitations, of science in relation to technical, social and economic development

and

> be concerned for the application of scientific knowledge within the community.

*From Geography 14–18; a Handbook for School-Based Curriculum Development. In this, the project team refers to 'aims', but these represent goals in terms of the terminology adopted here.

These are bound to evoke many different reactions and interpretations from teachers. Thus, goals statements of this type would normally fail to convey to potential curriculum users a curriculum developer's intentions in a meaningful and readily interpretable form.

Under circumstances like the preceding, curriculum goals do not fulfil either of the two functions referred to above and, instead, assume the qualities of curriculum aims: they express views and sentiments which, it is hoped, will receive common agreement, but which essentially lack operational value. Indeed, one might argue that any attempt to develop these statements into more specific, operationalized objectives would result in an array of statements which no longer find common agreement and approval. This potential danger can obviously be avoided by the curriculum developer by not elaborating his intentions beyond the statement of broadly-based goals. Numerous examples exist to suggest that this is indeed fairly common practice.

Referring to the two main functions of goals identified above, the analysis of a wide range of curriculum projects reveals that the first of these functions (goals used as bases from which the curriculum developers formulate objectives) has a much lower incidence rate than the second function (goals introduced as 'staging posts' for the curriculum user to develop his own objectives). Even when curriculum planners attempt, as a matter of policy, to translate their curriculum goals into objectives (in the meaning of the term used here), the resulting statements frequently fall short of the requirement associated with genuine objectives, and instead retain the characteristics of curriculum goals (examples of this are evident from the North West Regional Curriculum Development Project). Only in some Open University courses, notably those in mathematics, are statements of curriculum goals followed by detailed specifications of students' learning outcomes which are classifiable as objectives. This reflects the importance of a clear and unambiguous communication of educational intentions to the student in situations where there is no teacher present (such situations occur in programmed learning, individualized learning, distance learning, etc.) and of a precise specification of learning outcomes to guide the student in his studies. Even here, although standards of expected attainment are included in the statements of objectives, it is sometimes stated that these indicate only 'minimum' attainment and that the interested student should extend himself beyond this level by further work—reading, discussion, attendance at tutorials, and so on.

The claim is sometimes made that curriculum aims, goals and objectives represent an important tool for the rational planning of curricula. In our analysis, we were unable to identify any curriculum projects which had fully adopted this approach to curriculum planning. Even those projects which placed much emphasis on the formulation and statement of aims and goals (few proceeded to the formulation of objectives in our sense of the word), did not adopt a totally 'behaviourist' outlook and frequently mixed behaviourist and non-behaviouristic statements of intent.

If recent curriculum development work is considered in a chronological sequence, a general trend can be noticed concerning the use of aims and goals. It appears that early curriculum projects (those initiated in the early and mid-sixties) leant significantly more strongly towards the specification of students' learning outcomes than many of the more recent projects. This is partly explained by the general movement over this period of time from large-scale national projects producing fully tested, fairly rigidly designed 'curriculum packages' to curriculum proposals with a high degree of in-built flexibility and demanding teacher participation in both planning and realization. Another possible explanation for this trend is that many of the early projects concerned subjects and disciplines which, by the very nature, allow desirable student outcomes to be specified and formulated in terms of goals and objectives. [. . .]

There can be no doubt that the various statements of curriculum intentions associated with curricula reflect the curriculum developers' assumptions not only about the purpose of their curriculum but also about the nature of the subject to which the curriculum relates and about teaching and learning. For example, curricula in subjects which are considered to have a linear, hierarchical structure (i.e. involve a progression of concepts from a low to a sophisticated level, as, for example, in science, mathematics and modern languages), a predominance of statements is observed which express the acquisition and use of concepts. This emphasis on concepts tends to be further reinforced when the intellectual ability of the students for whom the curriculum is designed is perceived as high: in general, the higher the ability of the student, the greater is the stress on concepts. This results in a more 'academic' curriculum. By comparison, where the goals/objectives statements place greater emphasis on the processes inherent in a subject, this usually points to a curriculum which has a lower theoretical (academic) orientation and may, therefore, be suitable either for lower ability groups or for younger learners. This is the case in two recent science curricula: the Nuffield Working with Science project, designed for the non-academic sixth former; and the Schools Council Science 5–13 project which caters for junior and middle school pupils of all abilities.

Most of the subject-orientated goals expressed in recent curricula lean rather heavily on the epistemological make-up of the subject/discipline to which the curriculum relates. Thus, the emphasis in craft, design and technology curricula is on practical skills and the acquisition of creative skills and aesthetic values, whilst in mathematics, for example, intellectual abilities receive high priority. Subjects such as geography and history stress the understanding to be gained by the learner of the world surrounding him as it has been shaped, and is being shaped, by human events and interventions.

Two Contrasting Curriculum Models

Some Theoretical Considerations

In the introduction to this chapter, reference was made to the two main ways in which curriculum intentions may be expressed by curriculum developers. The first of these involves the detailed specification and elaboration of student's learning outcomes (which are often stated in behavioural terms), whilst the second focuses on the elaboration of teaching approaches and learning conditions to be created by the teacher. Though frequently both forms of expressing curriculum intentions are used simultaneously, it is nevertheless possible to detect biases and orientations towards either the one or other direction.

The two contrasting philosophies about how to express educational intentions give rise to two different approaches to curriculum planning which may be referred to as objectives-based and process-based, respectively. Objectives-based curricula are those in which the specification of desirable learning outcomes is central to the curriculum developer's task and where such statements of learning outcomes form an important reference against which the tenability of educational actions in the classroom must be judged. Process-based curricula, in contrast, focus on a clear description and identification of the pedagogical activities to be pursued and educational conditions to be established by the curriculum user, and these are seen as vital for the curriculum to be effective in terms of its broad aims.

The salient features of the two models may be broadly summarized as follows:

The objectives model

(i) Curricula developed on the basis of this model always stress intended educational outcomes in terms of learner achievement. These intentions are in the form of aims (learning aims), goals and objectives. In theory, at least, curricular experiences and materials developed for the student will serve the function of leading him/her to the attainment of these educational goals and objectives, and the success of a curriculum can be gauged from the extent to which the learner acquires the predetermined abilities, skills and attitudes.

(ii) Whilst the pedagogical activities of the teacher are sometimes suggested, they do not appear as the predominant feature of the curriculum specification but are mainly seen as means whereby the intended curriculum outcomes can be achieved. However, the implicit assumption is usually that such outcomes may be achieved by different means. However, sometimes the nature of the specified goals/objectives will demand particular types of learning experience to be arranged for the student.

(iii) This model is generally associated with subject-centred curricula and, by implication, with curricula employing intradisciplinary (i.e. 'within-a-discipline') integration. Its use is particularly in evidence in curricula where the subject matter involves the hierarchial ordering of concepts (linear subjects), as is the case for most mathematics and academic science curricula, as well as for curricula in the modern languages.

The process model

(i) the key feature of curricula based on this model is that they focus on teacher activities, pedagogical actions and on the nature of the teacher's role and, in addition, on conditions for instruction to be created. In this way, the nature of the learning experience is defined to which students are to be exposed, rather than the specific learning outcomes to be achieved from them. The assumption underlying this is that the prescribed learning experiences and pedagogical action provide the appropriate means of achieving the broad intentions of the curriculum.

(ii) Although in curricula developed on the basis of the process model broad indications may be given of the intended outcomes in the form of aims, curriculum goals and objectives as such tend not to be stated. Implicit in this is the assumption that the outcomes to be derived from the educational experiences cannot be described in any precise way in behavioural terms because the learner may make an unique and personalized response to that experience. This would be the case in relation to, for example, the acquisition of personality values, the development of self-realization, and so on. In these instances, the attainment of the broad educational intentions can manifest itself in many different behavioural patterns.

(iii) The process model of curriculum planning is prevalent mainly in curricula which are designed to teach social and life skills and in which the development of personal values and attitudes is particularly stressed. Many of the humanities curricula reflect this orientation as, indeed, do curricula in which an extensive interdisciplinary (i.e. 'across-the-disciplines') integration is attempted. In the latter cases, it is generally impossible to arrive at a consensus view about the conceptual content of what would be loosely defined study areas, and this would seem to shift the focus away from a specification of desirable student characteristics towards the prescription of teacher activities and pedagogical strategies. Indeed, a bias towards the process model seems in evidence whenever a study area lacks an agreed conceptual content, and this applies generally to 'non-linear' subjects.

Conclusions

The history of curriculum development shows that objectives-based approach to curriculum planning has distinct advantages in that the purposeful character of education can be overtly acknowledged. The strengths of the objectives model are at their most obvious when students' desired learning outcomes are readily definable in operationally meaningful terms. This is the case for curricula with a strong 'academic' orientation, especially in subjects or subject areas which may be considered 'linear' in terms of their conceptual content.

However, considerable difficulties arise when the objectives model is adhered to in situations in which personalized responses to learning situations are encouraged or where the emphasis is on development of affective characteristics, in addition to cognitive ones. Basically, the objectives model then becomes inadequate because any attempt to formulate meaningful statements in terms of student outcomes is doomed to failure since those statements inevitably lack operationality and any in-built criteria against which their attainment can be assessed.

A frequent response to this kind of situation is to reject the measurement of personality qualities, attitudes, and so on, on pragmatic grounds because there is no obviously satisfactory method of organizing such a measurement. The formulation of statements having the characteristics of goals and objectives becomes impossible and increasing emphasis is just put on the statement of aims. However, because these lack specificity and operationality, they have to be reinforced by prescription and recommendations for teacher activity and learning conditions. In this way, the objectives model is essentially abandoned and replaced by the process model, occasionally by a 'mixed model' which has elements of the objectives model and the process model.

The abandonment of the objectives model in favour of the process model should not be equated with an abandonment of educational goals as such. Despite the emphasis on the specification teacher activities, there is an implicit acknowledgement even in this model that there must necessarily be student outcomes. However, these outcomes are left unspecified because it is acknowledged that there is a diversity of responses to result from the learning experiences created by the adoption of the specified instructional procedures, and/or because such outcomes are not measurable in any absolute way.

The rationale for not providing conditions for assessability is often that it is not desirable to measure student behaviour because of the overtones of conformity and uniformity or that it distorts the nature of knowledge to do so. Some critics would, therefore, argue that the use of the process model is unacceptable because it invariably fails to provide the certification which students may need.

The history of curriculum development over the past two decades in secondary and higher education holds warnings for the curriculum developer in further education today. It reflects the danger of adopting a polarized stance on the use of curriculum models and on subsequently imposing a particular model without due regard for measurement and assessment issues in certain curriculum areas. Above all, it demonstrates the importance of choosing an appropriate model to serve the curriculum rather than forcing a curriculum into a model which may be totally unsuitable.

5

The British Disease: a British tradition?

MARGARET MATHIESON and GERALD BERNBAUM*

Introduction

The purpose of this article is to review and to analyse the contemporary rhetoric and practices which are increasingly dominating British education and whose influences are already being felt in significant organizational, financial and curricular changes, both in schools and in higher education. The general thrust of the most recent developments has, as its starting point, the inadequacy of British economic performance in the post-war period. That absolute decline and, above all, the relative decline consequent upon the emergence of major new international competitors, is seen by many to be due, in large part, to the failure of the education system which, it is argued, is divorced from the needs and problems of commerce and industry, and unresponsive to the demands of the market.

The major changes introduced over the last eight years (likely to be reinforced as a result of the outcome of the 1987 June election) involve, in essence, a major diminution of the influence and power of those groups who have traditionally been responsible for the administration of the education system in Britain. Professionals in the field of education are being faced with policies which attempt to transfer their power to the hands of groups, who, historically, have had little direct influence upon schooling or higher education. The government appears anxious to diminish local authority control of schools and, in turn, to extend its own direct influence through a variety of strategies involving the Department of Education and Science (DES) and a range of local commercial, industrial and parental groupings. At the same time, partly because senior members of government do not entirely trust the commitment of the educational establishment which, to a

*Source: From Mathieson, M. and Bernbaum, G. (1988) The British Disease: A British Tradition? *British Journal of Educational Studies*, Vol. XXVI No. 2. pp. 126–175.

degree, is embodied in the DES, newer agencies are being employed to act directly in a contractual fashion with schools and institutions of higher education, the most notable of which is the Manpower Services Commission (MSC), whose very large budget relates particularly to vocational and industrial training in its various forms. The MSC's policies of undertaking specific training initiatives, for which it invites educational institutions to bid for the resources, symbolize many of the current changes. Their aim is to make schools, universities and polytechnics more commercially aware, both with respect to the trained manpower they produce and with respect to their own day to day practices.

This article will argue, however, that many of the critics of contemporary British education are only repeating long standing anxieties about its nature and organization. For over the last hundred years there have been intermittent periods of critical analysis which have drawn attention to the greater success of other nations' educational institutions in producing pupils and students who are well prepared to meet commercial, industrial and scientific needs. Additionally it will argue that the relative failure of earlier critics to introduce effective reforms cannot be ignored. Their failure stands as a monument to the outstanding success of the British education system in embodying and perpetuating the values of British society's dominant elites. It should serve to instruct contemporary critics and reformers who ignore those long standing, deep rooted structural features of British society which have been responsible for the development of the educational system. Too many past reforming efforts have failed because the educational system has been viewed as a discrete unit, whose personnel act independently of other institutional arrangements in society and are supposedly uninfluenced by the values of its elites. Our purpose is not to criticize the present drive for reform. It is to place it in a context which treats the current prescriptions and recommendations as themselves problematic, and as being at risk precisely because the level of analysis from which they begin is inadequate. A more complex, and historically aware, analysis might perhaps, enable a somewhat different view to be taken of recent concerns and recommendations and hence of their likelihood of success where so many others have previously failed. [. . .]

We shall attempt to show how the dominant characteristics of the educational system which emerged during the nineteenth century reflected the nature of British society and its leading figures' responses to the phenomena of industrialization and urbanization. Central to our argument is that an arts based, Christian notion of gentlemanliness, which excludes, and even opposes science, technology and commerce, dominated high status educational institutions in the nineteenth century. This literary, Christian notion both reflected and consolidated the values of Victorian society, which conferred the highest status upon the ownership of land and the style and manners associated with gentlemanly distance both from the daily labours on that land and from what was regarded as the sordid features of industrialization and urbanization. Special emphasis will be placed upon this antipathetic response to science and technology which was, and continues to be, represented in the values embodied both in an arts based curriculum and in the relationship of the education system to other parts of society. We shall discuss, in particular, the relationship between the literary curriculum which dominated nineteenth century education and the writings of a significant group of authors, of whom Samuel Taylor Coleridge was the most influential. We shall focus upon their attempts to resist changes brought about by industrialization by asserting an essentially artistic, creative view of human spirit. Such an approach will lead us to conclude that the contemporary problems of this country which are currently being perceived as, to a large degree, attributable to the failure of the educational system are more adequately described as persistent characteristics of British society. We shall suggest that the foremost critics are, in many important ways, both products and victims of the very arrangements which they believe they are about to replace.

Education and the Economy: Contemporary Views

Foremost amongst the critics of the educational system are leading industrialists and those associated with training manpower for industrial roles. They complain bitterly about pupils' and students' 'low standards' in the central areas of English and mathematics and about their lack of enthusiasm and preparation for the worlds of industry and commerce. [. . .]

Moreover, industrialists' and politicians' general and specific dissatisfactions are enthusiastically reported and widely echoed in the national press which, during recent years, has persistently expressed hostility to teachers, schools and higher education. The education system is held uniquely and exclusively responsible both for the low standards of its products and for their unreadiness for the working conditions of contemporary industrial society. Other countries' success is attributed to the keen competitiveness, rigorous discipline and hard headed instrumentalism in their educational institutions. Britain's economic failure, it is claimed, is the fault of teachers and teacher educators who irresponsibly refuse to adopt realistic measures and attitudes. [. . .]

In all of this there are simple underlying assumptions which will not bear very close inspection. The relative decline of modern Britain is rooted in historical factors of great complexity, many of which are beyond the control of the nation's leaders and people. Contemporary critics of our educational institutions are guilty, not only of failing to acknowledge these external factors, but of being insensitive to the role of elite education in Britain in producing pupils and students who are unprepared for the needs of a modern industrial society. It is that elite education, its structure, processes, values and products which must be central to this present analysis and which can only be properly understood within its specific historical context. [. . .]

What unites all investigators of Britain's economic plight, whichever particular perspective they adopt, is an agreement that management and the managers of British industry have contributed to the decline of that industry. They comment upon two particular but inter-related features; firstly the failure of British industry to attract the brightest and best of each generation, and secondly the lack of sensitivity, imagination and technical expertise amongst those who eventually take up leadership roles in British industry. This perspective, we suggest, should not be seen as one which is merely to be regretted. It should be seen, rather, as an important illustration of the nature of elite education in industrial Britain. It was Martin Weiner who was the first, in a scholarly and sustained fashion, to draw attention to the disjunction between the workaday world of industry and that offered in the elite institutions of the Victorian pattern. In his words, these 'reflected and propagated an anti-industrial bias'. He refers to an Oxford science don in the first decade of this century who observed that this university had 'always ostentatiously held itself aloof from manufacturers and commerce'. Weiner reminds us that Sir Ernest Barker, himself a scholar of very humble origin, could nevertheless deplore what he perceived as the advent of courses in universities related to industrial needs. Barker feared lest universities degenerate into 'handy' institutions providing 'even the world of business with recruits'. According to Barker, the ancient universities had a special duty to defend the 'stronghold of pure learning' and 'long time values against the demands of material progress'.[1] As recently as 1958 a vice-chancellor, quoted by Weiner, observed with telling adjectival contempt that 'the crude engineer, the mere technologist are tolerated in universities because the state and industry are willing to finance them, tolerated but not assimilated'. It is easy to multiply such sentiments. Roderick and Stephens, in *Where Did We Go Wrong?* make similar points,[2] whilst Pollard observes, towards the end of his analysis of British economic failure, that 'among the permissive causes affecting the British economy adversely is the frequently discussed weakness in applied science and engineering. The low status of these subjects has its roots in history and . . . implies a preference for "gentlemanly" arts subjects in the training of entrepreneurs . . .'. Pollard goes on to argue that 'the essence of the British problem lies in the inability of the engineering profession to reach in any numbers the highest echelons of power in private industry as well as in government'.[3]

The Nineteenth Century: Religion and Literature

It is to the unique characteristics of British society and its emergent educational institutions during the nineteenth century that we now address ourselves. Central to our discussion is the religious, arts based intellectual concept of gentlemanliness which developed in response to anxieties about perceived threats to the quality of society consequent upon industrialization and urbanization. This concept controlled elite educational institutions in the nineteenth century and continues to dominate British society and education today. [. . .]

Victorian headmasters' enthusiasm for the moral virtues, which they believed to be realisable through Christianity, the study of the Classics and the corporate life of the school, derived partly from the values associated with the style and manners of the country's great landowners.

Part of our argument is that it is the success of Victorian liberals' crusade against science, under the banner of literature, which goes far towards explaining the apparent 'failure' of today's schools and universities. It needs to be fully recognized that Coleridge's concept of the clerisy, an educated, literary elite with the special responsibility to diffuse the virtues associated with religion and literary culture throughout society, penetrated the writings of Thomas and Matthew Arnold and extends through liberal theorists in England to F. R. Leavis and to contemporary supporters of literature and the arts. Coleridge's views underpinned their convictions about the superiority of literature, the artistic imagination and religion over science and technology in the education system, most particularly in the education of the nation's elite. The way in which these views have been carried forward into this century has been of great importance in all the debates about the nature of the school curriculum and about the kind of provision which should be made available in teacher training establishments [. . .]

Anti-scientific and anti-commercial attitudes, as these derived from the coalescence of aristocratic land owning values and Coleridge's clerisy theory, penetrated the attitudes of the nation's leaders in every area of national life.

It is a major part of our concern to demonstrate how the shared gentlemanly values of aristocratic landowners, Victorian headmasters, and educational theorists who advocated the supremacy of the literary curriculum succeeded in establishing a dominant literary elite in English society. The potency of their success will become evident in the next section where we discuss the contrasting fates of the two major challenges made to it, firstly by science and technology and secondly by progressive, child centred education. Proponents of scientific and technical education failed to bring about significant and lasting changes at any level of education. Supporters of progressive child centred education, however, from Edmond Holmes, through Sir Percy Nunn, to David Holbrook, achieved a remarkable degree of success in converting the Inspectorate to their views, even though it was not until the nineteen sixties that these were given serious consideration. A major factor in their success, in contrast with those attempting seriously to introduce science and technology into education, was the progressive educators' belief in the educational and spiritual value of the arts. The early progressive educators in England, most particularly, Edmond Holmes, Inspector of Schools, and author of the seminal text, *What Is and What Might Be: The Path to Self Realization*, shared European and American contemporaries' distrust of traditional educational institutions, of the centrality of texts and of adult authority. They, too, strove to redirect teachers' attention to the unique nature of childhood and of every different child, to his capacity for inner directed growth to self realization. They all believed in the crucial importance of interest, enjoyment and direct, active, first hand experiences under the guidance of loving teachers in children's learning and development. Drawing upon the developmental theories of Rousseau, Froebel, Pestalozzi and Herbart, progressive educators placed the child at the centre of the learning process, asserting the goal of personal 'wholeness' in education and advocating 'play', most particularly through experiences of things rather than words, in every child's growth. What distinguished progressive educators in England from their European and American counterparts, however, was, and continues to be, their conviction about the special role of the arts, most especially children's artistic creativity, in the achievement of self realization. Unlike progressive educators abroad, who also repudiated the elitism and irrelevance of nineteenth-century schools' concern with words rather than things, and proposed that 'learning by discovery' take place according to the empirical scientific model, the parallel movement in England invested its keenest reforming enthusiasm in the arts, especially children's creative writing. Although progressive educators in England rejected the means whereby the clerisy theorists sought to achieve their spiritual and moral goals through Classical tests, institutionalized religion and competitive team games, they share the conservatives' deep distaste for science and industry, their respect for spiritual and moral, rather than intellectual, virtues and their special attachment to the English countryside. Like the conservatives they were powerfully influenced by the Romantic poets, especially Coleridge, and viewed literature as having a specially educative function. But their convictions about the joyous, intuitive, visionary and creative nature of childhood, and the crucial role of imaginative activity, derived from his theories of the active mind which meshed persuasively with their progressive educational notions.

The continuity of the Coleridgean tradition well into this century has been, we argue, a major influence upon both the public schools and the nature of state education as it developed in the elementary schools and the secondary schools which were gradually provided through rates and taxes. Definitions of education persisted which emphasized Christianity in its religious mode and high morality in its secular mode. For the mass of children, discipline and good behaviour became the dominant themes. For a few, intellectual achievement could be emphasized, but only of a kind which seemingly allowed entry into a latter day clerisy, through the Classics and literature. Even the penetration of progressive educational ideas after the First World War, and their revival in the nineteen sixties, did little to alter those basic conditions. For progressive education itself became defined in terms of the spirit and the imagination. Whichever way one turns, therefore, technical, scientific and vocational education occupy inferior positions. The buttress to all this was, of course, the maintenance of the gentlemanly ideal as we have discussed it within the major schools.

It is interesting to contrast, throughout this century, the outcome of the progressive challenge to the classical literary experience. As we have already noted, unlike the scientific and technological challenge, it was able to find a place in the pantheon of values emanating from the civilizing missions of the schools and their teachers. Although the present educational climate is hostile to the perceived excesses of child centred learning, official opinion, until very recently, has been far more receptive to progressive educational notions than to recommendations about science and technology. By the end of the nineteenth century the political, spiritual and cultural problems of disorder, disunity and personal isolation which troubled Coleridge and his successors appeared to conservative and progressive educators alike to have worsened. Sir James Shelley, a leading advocate of progressive educational approaches, spoke for many troubled observers of modern, urban industrial conditions when he wrote in 1919 that:

> The terrible negation, and even destruction, of millions of potential human beings by employing them as mechanical cogs in the industrial machine, is the most inhuman form of tyranny I can imagine, and there seems to be no escape from it except by adopting a life of crime.[4]

Progressive educators insisted that the traditional classical curriculum in the public schools and merely useful knowledge in the elementary schools were both failing to engage pupils in the learning process which should be fostering their personal growth. They maintained, moreover, that traditional teaching methods encouraged competitiveness rather than co-operation and conformity rather than originality: these twin evils, they insisted, exacerbated the problems of divisiveness and fragmentation in wider society. The progressives, therefore, urged teachers to find ways of making education a more meaningful experience for pupils at every level to compensate for the feared pernicious effects of increasing industrialization, urbanization and, a new threat, cheap entertainment. Sharing the conservatives' faith in the educative value of literature, especially poetry, they transferred their hopes from exclusive concentration upon books in schools to what they were convinced was every child's own capacity for artistic, creative expression. [. . .]

Rejecting dismissively any attempts to apply objective criteria in the evaluation of children's writing, Abbs reminds teachers of their special task in an area which inevitably remains outside the conventional assessments made in school of children's work. Demanding of the teachers of expressive arts that they have confidence in their unique and crucial role, he reminds them that:

> . . . creative writing is concerned with the expression of the whole person. Let us not murder it before it exists. Let us not worry over details of formal correctness; nor let us worry about assessing it. If the work is good and embodies the unique, it cannot be marked, it cannot be compared to anything beyond itself. There can be no objectivity. In which case why bother? Why lie?[5]

Such views have persisted in sections of the prescriptive writing about English since the end of the Second World War and are currently being expressed with passion by those who are opposed to what is viewed as the recommendations of soulless vocationalism in education. The artistic thrust of this country's progressive educational movement was, moreover, greatly strengthened by the desire of many theorists to revive, in schools, the lost folk culture which, it was believed, preceded industrialization. From the influential 'Cambridge School' of teachers and writers came persistent recommendations for less academic pupils, as well as the very young, to 'grow' and, consequently, to 'resist' the corrupting features of modern urban industrialism, through creative artistic experiences. [. . .]

What made it especially easy for progressive educators in the British mode to find a place within the rhetoric and ideology of the older school was their common attachment to certain central convictions. Thus, there was their shared anti-industrialism and belief in the virtues of nature and in earlier, pre-industrial communities. Similarly, though not all the progressive educators shared the religiosity of the clerical conservatives, they nevertheless held strongly to a range of secular moral beliefs which derived from the Judeo-Christian tradition and which certainly, as we have demonstrated, embodied the view of schools and of teachers as carrying light into dark places.

The Romantic protest against the Enlightenment in England has, therefore, resulted in persistent conservatism in this country's educators, traditionalists and progressives alike. No serious challenge has succeeded in displacing official faith in an arts based curriculum believed to be creative of pupil's superior moral health and a cohesive sense of community.

It could be argued, of course, that what has characterized the last eight or nine years has been the way in which older values, particularly those established within the landed groups in the Tory party, have been diminished, and may even have been destroyed, by the newer form of conservatism, which is radical and technical and pragmatic in its orientation. It could be argued that the Prime Minister and her closest associates do not come, literally or metaphorically, from the old school, and that their social origins and predilections make them better able to implement reformist policies aimed at reconstructing British industry and business, to a degree, at least, through education and training. Putting the case for the 'core curriculum' in *The Times*, John Rae argued

> For the first time, a British government is openly espousing the idea that there is a direct connection between the curriculum and the health—in our case the economic health—of society . . . Kenneth Baker will be assuring Parliament that a national curriculum is necessary to bring about the economic regeneration of Britain.[6]

Such optimism, we suggest, may be premature at a time when a leading figure in the same Establishment, Sir Bryan Nicholson, could, with confidence, equate the science and technology within this reformed curriculum in modern Britain with 'the spanner and the spark plug'.

References

1. Weiner, M. J. (1981) *English Culture and the Decline of the Industrial Spirit 1850–1980*, Cambridge University Press, Cambridge, p. 133.
2. Roderick, G. and Stephens, M. (1981) *Where Did We Go Wrong?* The Falmer Press, Falmer, p. 25.
3. Pollard, S. (1982) *The Wasting of the British Economy*, Croom Helm, Beckenham, p. 160.
4. Shelley, J. (1909) *What do we mean by freedom for the Child?* CEA.
5. Abbs, P. (1969) *English for Diversity*, Heinemann, London, p. 52.
6. Rae, John (1987) Putting the Case for the Core, *The Times*, 11 September.

6

What Hopes for Liberal Education?

CHARLES BAILEY*

How should an advocate of liberal education read the signs and portents of the times? Is our age one of hope or despair for liberal educators? These are, of course, different questions from those about the content, justification and methodology of liberal education, being less philosphical and more matters of observational judgement. It is not so much a matter of trying to argue that liberal education *should* be of such and such a kind and *should* prevail, which I have done in other places,[1] as trying to speculate whether the influences creating, sustaining and seeking to expand liberal education are likely or not to be overcome by the forces acting against such a view of education. Reading the entrails on social and political matters is a messy business, and not only so because of the metaphor. Unless the observer operates within a closed system of social analysis—some form of Marxism, for example, or uncritical assumptions about the rights of the free market—he is forced to admit that the mesh of forces and influences under scrutiny cannot be assessed by tests of logic, coherence and reason simply because what is happening often appears arbitrary, incoherent and unreasonable to the observer, but is nevertheless indubitably happening! We make subjective guesses about how things are likely to go, based on such information as we are able to seek out or comes our way.

Yet although all that sounds very unsatisfactory the making of such judgements is a necessity for the liberal educator in order to know the circumstances and contexts within which he or she is likely to be operating. At the extreme we need to know whether the struggle—if it is to be a struggle—is reasonably worth continuing. More moderately we need to know the extent and limits of the personal space in which we might continue to operate as liberal educators if, as I am assuming here, that is what we wish to do. Without some assurance that at least some such personal and professional space will continue to exist the position of a

*Source: From Bailey, C. (1988) *Cambridge Journal of Education*, Vol. 18 No. 1, pp. 27–37.

liberal educator simply becomes untenable. Marxists, of course, have always argued that in a capitalist society this is necessarily the case: teachers who consider themselves liberal educators are idealists simply ignorant of the real forces determining their professional actions, fooling themselves as to the actual consequences of their teaching.[2] I have argued elsewhere that whilst this view is not entirely without foundation the way in which it is often put is grossly exaggerated and unnecessarily defeatist.[3] The number of teachers adopting the Marxist view is not surprisingly small, very small indeed in my experience; but one does encounter a much larger number of teachers who reject the possibilities of liberal education on grounds that they see as less theoretical, more pervasive and more directly bearing on their daily professional lives. These teachers perceive, correctly I think, at least three powerful pressures of a quite different kind which always constrain, and at the worst defeat, their endeavour to liberally educate their pupils. These pressures are seen as coming from public examinations and the increased numbers of pupils being prepared for them; from a dominant and pervasive view of education as mainly instrumental or vocational in its aims; and the increasing reality of central government influence through its powerful agencies of persuasion, its allocation of finance, its desire to control the curriculum and its intention to institute forms of targeting and testing. Taken together these pressures are seen by many as leaving teachers little, if any, of the personal and autonomous space that is necessary to act as liberal educators.

Before looking more closely at these constraining influences there is a less obvious point which arises. It is a matter of some importance in the national education of children how teachers see their role in that system. A liberal education requires teachers who are confident and enthusiastic bearers of intellectual disciplines and traditions of inquiry, with an unalloyed loyalty to these disciplines and to the pupils who are to be initiated into them and to *nothing* else. If teachers, subject to the attrition generated by a variety of vested interests start to see themselves as simply the possessors of neutral pedagogic skills which are placed at the service of the most powerful, then to that extent they can no longer operate as liberal educators. The vision, the coherence and even the excitement of the educators' profession is inexorably worn away in the confusing difficulty of following conflicting wishes and the demoralizing effect of constant failure to satisfy these external, changeable and multifarious wishes. The observational evidence does seem to show some teachers who are more or less content with this conception of their role, looking anxiously all the time to discern and keep up with the latest expectations from without. But the same observation shows other teachers clearly discontented and frustrated by the role they see others as forcing them into. They see themselves as being told by the politically powerful that it is not really the responsibility of the teacher to have any overall view of what education is properly about; that is for others to determine, and it is the task of the teacher to implement the wishes of these others. There is thus, on this view, little incentive for a teacher to engage in the kind of reflection and intellectual inquiry that provides the basis, the groundwork of assumptions, for liberal education and liberal educators. It is hardly to be wondered at that a disparaging of ideals, a contempt for and a disregard of theoretical study and a sapping of intellectual will and energy are increasingly encountered among teachers. I suspect, though in these matters of observational judgement one might clearly be wrong, that the running discontent of teachers over the last few years has been little to do with salary matters, except in the sense that our society increasingly signals respect and significance in monetary terms. The old and characteristic insult of our society: 'If you are so smart why ain't you rich?' bears sharply on teachers! The real discontents, however, lie deeper than this, deriving from the role confusions and the lack of focus of a proper professional loyalty, pride and responsibility mentioned above.

Nothing that can be said about teachers, however, applies to all. There are devoted liberal educators to be found, still optimistically believing that they can prevail, at least to some extent, within the three great constraints indicated above. How justifiable is such optimism?

Public examinations at 16 + and 18 + are seen as constraining liberal educators in three ways. First by encouraging early concentration by students on a narrowing range of intellectual concerns; secondly by a determination of syllabus in a way that bears externally on particular pupils and teachers; and thirdly by the difficulty of teaching in a critical and evidential way when extensive content has to be covered. These constraints, teachers claim, make wide and genuine intellectual engagement difficult, for both pupils and teachers, and foster a kind of inauthentic academicism, a guessing game in which the object is mainly one of anticipating and beating the snares of the examiners.[4] Remember we are talking about the perceptions of pupils and teachers. These perceptions guide their actions and are not readily changed by simple assertions on the part of syllabus-makers and examiners that their intentions are wrongly perceived. The examination ethos and perceived purpose has proved inordinately difficult to change. As the number of pupils taking public examinations of one kind or another has increased so the anti-liberal effect of the ethos has simply become more widespread. Liberal features which educators try to build into the system are either strangled at birth or worn away by the difficulty of accommodating them to the general purposes of the system. An example of the 'strangling at birth' type is to be seen in the repeated refusal of universities to accept any alteration at 18 + which would allow 16–18-year-old students to study across a wider range of subjects, especially across the arts-science divide. Such a widening is seen by many educators as extremely important if 'civilized society' is to mean a society in which choices about the use of technology are made in humanistic ways. Such a society requires a considerable understanding of *both* technology *and* humanistic studies by as many people as possible. We continue our failure to achieve this necessity of a liberal society largely because of the constraints of the examinations system. An example of the 'wearing away' type would be the fate of Mode 3 in the now discarded CSE examination. This was an interesting attempt to blend the educational purposes of a course based on internally derived syllabuses with the need to externally moderate for comparative purposes. But Mode 3 always lodged unhappily in the general examination ethos, and never became dominant in spite of its reasonable rationale.

Will GCSE be more or less liberal in its effect? If one looks at the National Criteria across a range of subjects there seems little doubt of liberal intentions. The important relationship between actual pupil and actual teacher is seen to be valued in the emphasis given to coursework and its marking. Evidential teaching and learning is frequently and commonly indicated; imagination and depth of understanding appear to be favoured in a number of criteria; it is recognized that not all educational aspirations are translatable into assessment objectives; and there appears to be a genuine attempt to make assessment criteria as educational as possible. One could carp at some things: behavioural objectives seem to be very influential still in spite of the criticisms of such objectives in the seventies;[5] some objectives have a distinct air of over-ambition;[6] and there remains a doubt in many minds that the aspirations embodied in the criteria are realisable within the available resources. Nevertheless there is hope for liberal educators in GCSE and they should support its endeavours. At the very least it creates a framework within which liberal educators can work and argue. With energy, resources and continuing good will it could be much more than that.

To turn to the second of the perceived constraints, that of the pervasive pressure of an instrumental view of education, is to consider a constraint that is powerful, often quite overt, but also sometimes quite subtle in its manifestations. The view of the liberal educator is straightforward: schools of general education should not be places of vocational training. In spite of considerable pressure in the direction of vocational education in recent years it is probably still possible to make the empirical claim that our schools are not *de facto* places of vocational training. Even some supporters of the Technical and Vocational Education Initiatives (TVEI) have come to argue that its intention, methodology and effect is essentially liberal,[7] thereby accepting liberal education criteria as appropriate in judging it. Although the picture is varied it is probably true that in terms of its teaching and learning strategies, and in terms of the understanding that can be engendered within its framework, TVEI is often more liberal than some of us had feared it might be. So far, from the liberal educator's point of view, so good!

This, however, is not the end of the concern. TVEI remains an important, well-financed and powerful reinforcement of a view of education which does seem not only to stand opposed to the idea of liberal education but to make the aims of liberal educators more difficult to achieve. This view judges education very largely, and often solely, in terms of its contribution to the earning capacity of individuals and those they will, if lucky, work for and, on a wider canvas, to the wealth creating capacity of the nation. Such a view has characterized many political statements on education in recent years and continues to do so. It was largely because education appeared to be failing the country *in these terms* that pressures of a vocational kind, like TVEI, were placed on the schools, partly by the stick and partly by the very persuasive financial carrot.[8] Thus, in spite of his liberal claims for TVEI, Ron Wallace, then a county TVEI director, was quite clear that:

> Its prime object was to explore ways of managing the curriculum, so that more young people end their formal education at 18 with vocationally relevant qualifications. Projects are well funded . . . (and) financed and controlled by the Manpower Services Commission.[9]

A primarily vocational view of education has probably always been widespread among parents and pupils themselves. Youth unemployment, far from weakening this view, has tended to strengthen it. If education does not help a youngster to get a job then there must be something wrong with the education provided. Indeed, David Young (now Lord Young) appeared at one time to be directly blaming teachers and the schools for the rise in youth unemployment. It is not the purpose of this article to demonstrate the shortcomings of such a crude utility view of education.[10] Our present concern is its prevalence and power. Any teacher who can demonstrate to pupils and parents the vocational point of a learning activity is on a good wicket; but by the same token teachers of poetry, literature, music, art, and even moral and religious education appear increasingly vulnerable. To claim the value of these and other educational activities as basically intrinsic is, of course, correct, but such a claim cuts little ice in a society where wealth creation looks more and more like an end in itself. Motivating pupils in school in these areas of the curriculum becomes difficult because for most pupils there is no reinforcement in society at large or in the home. Attempting to provide or stimulate motivation by tortuously claiming some vocational spin-off for everything is clearly seen as at best specious; at its worst it is simply destructive of the really humane values we seek to encourage. No wonder that in this area of constraint there is little of encouragement to liberal educators in recent developments.

How do the proposals for a compulsory national curriculum fit into this scenario? Do they threaten liberal educators? In considering the possible constraints of central control there are really two issues. Most of the discussion about the recent clutch of government proposals has focused on the content of the proposals, i.e. in the case of the national curriculum on the proposed core and foundation subjects as to whether they are the right ones. There is, however, the prior question of the justification of any determination of these matters by central government at all. John Stuart Mill was sure that such central control and direction is not justified. The State, according to Mill, should enforce education but not determine its nature:

> The objections which are urged with reason against State education do not apply to the enforcement of education by the State, but to the State's taking upon itself to direct that education; which is a totally different thing.[11]

It is possible to argue, however, that Mill's position, whilst honourably libertarian, is not quite coherent. If it is important that the provision of education is to be enforced this must be because of some value or worthwhileness seen in education. If this is so it could not be the case that *anything* called 'education' will do. There must be a distinctive kind of education in mind such that certain offers would not even count as education. It then follows that it would not be unreasonable for a democratically elected government to require schools to provide the distinctive kind of education deemed to be worthwhile. All then hinges on the justification of the kind of education to be enforced. A government can claim a duty not only to ensure that all children are educated, but that all children are educated in some justifiable kind of way. By the same token, however, a government abrogates its right to direct education to the extent that the kind of education enforced is not justifiable. I have argued elsewhere,[12] and so have others,[13] that the very presuppositions on which democracy rests require the education of the young to have a rational and critical autonomy as its aim. Such an aim is the aim of liberal education. The claim would therefore be, on this view, that a government has some justification, indeed it exercises a duty, in requiring schools to provide a liberal education in some clearly characterized way. A government has no right on the same argument, though of course it might well have the power, to impose any other kind of education.

The scrutiny of the proposals for a National Curriculum is thus doubly important for liberal educators. First we are looking to see if the content proposals are liberal or otherwise; but secondly we are looking to see whether the government is operating in accord with its democratic rights and duties or in a way that is inconsistent with such entitlements and obligations.

There is, of course, no clear expression of liberal intent in the discussion document.[14] Indeed, it is easy to read the opposite. The expressed intention is:

> to secure for all pupils in maintained schools a curriculum which equips them with the knowledge, skills and understanding that they need for adult life and employment.[15]

And this still has the old familiar instrumental ring about it. Education is to consist of the kind of things it is useful, in our particular society, to know and to be able to do. This criterion, however, if applied to the list of proposed core and foundation subjects, does not seem to have imposed itself with any force or consistency. Contemporary 'needs' in our society could well be argued to include at least some knowledge, understanding and skill in politics, economics and finance, but these are not mentioned. The proposed curriculum content displays the same unargued arbitrariness that we have become used to in this kind of departmental document. It thus becomes easy to point to omissions in the list of foundation subjects, and many critics have already done this, especially in regard to moral education, religious education and personal and social education. In the pages of at least one national newspaper[16] we have seen the *cri de coeur* of the influential Latin lobby. This debate, which is of enormous national importance, is thus reduced to skirmishing between various vested interests because none of the parties to the debate wants to offer or challenge any coherent overall rationale for the total curriculum. One cannot challenge the basic principles of the document because there do not appear to be any—at least ones that can be declared. All one can do is pick the document over for helpful and unhelpful signs!

There are *hints* of a rationale in the document, and they are not in themselves illiberal. For example:

> . . . ensuring that all pupils study a broad and balanced range of subjects throughout their compulsory schooling and do not drop too early studies which may stand them in good stead later, and which will help to develop their capacity to adapt and respond flexibly to a changing world . . .[17]

expresses, albeit loosely, a liberal intent. Breadth of study *is* a liberal aspiration. The fundamentality and generality of studies necessary to 'adapt and respond flexibly' *are* at the heart of a liberal tradition. The implications of such a rationale are not worked out, however, in terms of the advocated content, or in anything else in the document. One is bound to read them as rhetoric. Similarly, the idea of the commonality of all worthwhile learning— the idea that such knowledge, understanding and skills as are genuinely worthwhile should be the right of 'all pupils, regardless of sex, ethnic origin and geographical location'[18] is clearly liberal. But again there is no further argument to support the view that the advocated content constitutes such a worthwhile package. We are up against rhetoric again. In the absence of any argument with which to contend one can only point out that the concern about omissions at least demonstrates that there is no prima facie obviousness, which seems to have been assumed, as to the justification of the list.

In summary, then, there are no principles of reason why a national curriculum required by a government for maintained schools should not and could not be liberal in intent, expression and effect. Sadly, there is also no reason to believe that what the present Government has in fact produced is anything of the kind.

There are some other questions to be asked about the present position of liberal education in the United Kingdom. One important strategic question is that of who is most likely to further the task of continuously creating and defending liberal education, or resisting such attacks and inroads as may be made upon it. This is, of course, one of those mixed 'is and ought' questions that thought about education always uncovers. It is not only a socialogical question about the sources of actual power to make and enact educational decisions, though it is partly and importantly at least that; but it is also a question of the duties and responsibilities that can justifiably be ascribed to different people in a national community. Thus the question is to do both with where power resides and where it properly or improperly resides. Further, as I have already argued in the case of the power of the state to impose a national curriculum, it is possible to argue that even when it is shown that a power is held by someone *de facto*, and even *de jure*, and that holding that power *can* be morally justifiable, the exercise of such power only remains justifiable whilst it is exercised in appropriate ways: rights over children, and all other persons for that matter, are never absolute.

Take the case of parents as an example. The rights of parents, in contemporary rhetoric at least, seem often to have a degree of paramountcy that hardly concurs with the socio-political factors or the justificatory logic. Parents not infrequently claim a right to have children reared and educated in a quite specific framework of belief and action which happens to be theirs. Bruce Ackerman has well argued that whilst the security of cultural homogeneity within the family is necessary in early childhood, parents have a duty not to prevent the later exposure of their children to a diversity of life-styles and belief systems. In particular, children should be free to attend schools of liberal education where there is at least the possibility, though of course not the certainty, that they might come to embrace beliefs and adopt actions not shared by their parents.[19] This is because the only common educational duty that bears on *all* parents is that they should seek the development of rational autonomy for their children, or at least not seek to hinder the development of that autonomy.[20] A similar line is taken in the Swann Report, though it is not so well articulated or argued. When the Report asserts:

> Education has to be something more than the reinforcement of the beliefs, values and identity which each child brings to school.[21]

and

> . . . it should also seek to develop in *all* pupils, both ethnic majority and minority, a flexibility of mind and an ability to analyse critically and rationally the nature of British society today within a global context.

it is making the claims of liberal education as against any particularist claims of parents.

Parents then, it can be and is argued, have a duty to seek the liberal education of their children. Can liberal educators therefore welcome any increase in actual parental power in education arising from the 1986 Act and the 1987 proposals? This is where argument ceases again and we return to speculation. For what we might call the Ackerman-Swann aspirations to be realized two conditions must obtain, quite apart from the force of the argument. First it must be the case that parents accept their liberal education duty; and secondly schools must actually operate as places of liberal education. Neither of these conditions obtains in any complete way.

Parents do not, of course, constitute a homogeneous group in terms of their educational aspirations. It is possible to find particular parents espousing a great variety of educational views. This variety is wider, I suspect, than will be found among any other group unless we count the population as a whole as one group. It would almost certainly be wider than that found among teachers and other professional educators. Nevertheless, within this variety there are very likely some dominant features, and one of these would be a strongly utilitarian, even mainly vocational, view of education. Twenty years ago it was possible for the then Schools Council to say:

> Both 15-year-old school-leavers and their parents very widely saw the provision of knowledge and skills which would enable young people to obtain the best jobs and careers of which they were capable as one of the main functions which a school should undertake. Teachers, however, rejected the achievement of vocational success as a major objective of education.[22]

John Raven, writing in 1977, reviewed the Schools Council Enquiry and two further major studies and commented:

> As we have already seen teachers do not share the pupil's orientation toward the more narrowly utilitarian, instrumental and vocational aspects of education. This difference is more marked in Britain than in Ireland. In both countries the orientation is shared by 15 to 17-year-old school-leavers. What we can now see is that, in Britain, parents go along with their children . . .[23]

These enquiries were based on a very large sample, 4,546 parents in the Schools Council Enquiry, and I know of nothing so large since. What *has* happened since is that the utilitarian view of education has received continuous support and advocacy from government agencies and most politicians; indeed, it would probably be more correct to say that this conception of education has been built into talk about education as though it was the only conceivable view. In addition to this, and supplementing its strategic force, we have seen a widening of assumptions about the rights of parents to choice and influence in education.

The consequence of all this is, I believe, that it would be as unreasonable for liberal educators to think that they will get much help or encouragement from enhanced parent power as it would be to expect such help from government or employers.

The other assumption of what I have called the Ackerman-Swann position is that schools of liberal education exist, the only problem being their equal access to all children. This, of course, is only partly true. It is not as false as some Marxists would have us believe, but still not wholly the case. Liberal educators still have much work to do in their schools before we could claim them truly to be places of liberal education.

By 'liberal educators' it must be increasingly clear that I mean those teachers in schools who see themselves as liberal educators. Such teachers, in the late eighties and into the nineties, seem likely to find few allies except one another. Even some powerful allies of the recent past, notably HMIs and local education authorities, are having their power and influence diminished in ways that would need a separate article to describe and analyse. The fact of this minority position is even used as an argument to demonstrate the wrongness of the liberal education point of view. It is no necessary part of democratic theory, however, that majorities must be right and minorities wrong. In a liberal democratic society the test is not whether a majority always has its way but, as recent writers like Rawls, Ackerman, Gewirth and Ratz[24] have shown, whether such a society acts on principles which would respect and enhance and continually recreate the personal autonomy on which ideas of democracy are founded—which democracy presupposes. Not only is this not a mere matter of majority rule; neither is it simply a matter of *laissez-faire*, the negative liberty of leaving people alone:

> There is more one can do to help another person have an autonomous life than stand off and refrain from coercing and manipulating him. There are two further categories of autonomy-based duties towards another person. One is to help in creating the inner capacities required for the conduct of an autonomous life. Some of these concern cognitive capacities, such as the power to absorb, remember and use information, reasoning abilities, and the like.[25]

Joseph Ratz writes too of the way in which emotion, imagination, ability to form personal attachment, physical abilities and skills, and the development of certain kinds of character traits all help towards autonomy. These, together with the creation of an adequate range of options for the person to choose from, constitute, for Ratz, the kinds of capacities members of a liberal democratic society have a duty to help one another acquire. He refers to a principle of autonomy, that is, 'the principle requiring people to secure the conditions of autonomy for all people'.[26]

Liberal educators, by definition, seek to help people become more autonomous. They do not, therefore, become bad democrats because, finding themselves in a minority with this aspiration, they continue professionally to seek ways in which they might further their aims. The bad democrats are those who would use their majority in ways that hinder the development and enhancement of personal autonomy. Such people continue to be bad democrats whether they are members of government, employers, parents or even pupils, themselves, whenever they make the task of liberal education more difficult, since by so doing they subvert the continuous creation and recreation of the very dispositions, knowledge and understanding on which democracy both rests and depends. What hope, then, for liberal educators? The pragmatically inclined will be pessimistic, for most of the objectively discernible forces leave little room for optimism. Liberal educators, however, are typically idealistic and properly so. They believe ideals to be necessary and their particular ideals to be justifiable and not arbitrary, and these thoughts encourage optimism and the will to continue to carry the torch. What is additionally necessary, perhaps, is that liberal educators themselves become much more adept at the argument, rhetoric and political action so well used by their recent opponents. This, of course, is no new idea: it was well understood in classical Athens, the historical birthplace of both liberal democracy and liberal education.

Correspondence: Charles Bailey, 24 Common Lane, Sawston, Cambridge, CB2 4HW, United Kingdom.

Notes and References

1. See Bailey, Charles (1984) *Beyond the Present and the Particular: a theory of liberal education* (London, Routledge & Kegan Paul). For discussion and criticism see Gibson, Rex (Ed.) (1986) *Liberal Education Today* (Cambridge, Cambridge Institute of Education). See also Bailey, Charles, Liberal education reconsidered, in Entwistle, Noel, [Ed.) *Handbook of Educational Ideas and Practices* (Beckenham, Croom Helm) (in press).
2. For a strong exposition of this view see Harris, Kevin (1979) *Education and Knowledge* (London, Routledge & Kegan Paul). See also Sharp, Rachel (1986) Social theory and social justice: the possibility of liberal education, in: Gibson, Rex (Ed.) op. cit.
3. Bailey, Charles: *Beyond the Present and the Particular* (Henceforth BPP) Chapter 10.
4. These observations are based mainly on my own talks with teachers on in-service courses. But see also Somekh, Bridget (1985) The relationship between examinations and teaching for understanding, in: Ebbutt, Dave & Elliott, John (Eds) (1985) *Issues in Teaching for Understanding* (Harlow, Longman for SCDC), and also other papers in that collection.
5. The most notable and consistently profound being those in many of the writings of the late Lawrence Stenhouse, the clearest of the critics of behavioural objectives.
6. For example the chemistry assessment objective, under 'understanding', which requires pupils to be able to 'explain the social, economic, environmental and technological implications of chemistry'! See GCSE: The National Criteria: Chemistry, p. 2.
7. Wallace, Ron: TVEI as liberal education, in: Gibson, Rex (Ed.), op. cit.
8. The stick was the threat to set up separate schools of a vocational kind outside the normal system. The financial carrot is well known.
9. Wallace, Ron, op. cit.
10. But see BPP, Chapter 9.
11. Mill, John Stuart: Essay on Liberty, Chap. 5. See p. 239 in the convenient Fontana paperback edited by Mary Warnock (1962).
12. BPP, pp. 225–228.
13. The clearest expositor of the connection between the principles that should govern the liberal state and the necessity for liberal education is to be found in Ackerman, Bruce (1980) *Social Justice and the Liberal State* (New Haven, Yale University Press). Other liberal political philosophers who convey the same idea include: Rawls, John (1971) *A Theory of Justice* (Oxford, OUP); Gewirth, Alan, (1978) *Reason and Morality* (Chicago, University of Chicago Press); Ratz, Joseph, (1986) *The Morality of Freedom* (Oxford, OUP).
14. Department of Education and Science (1987) *The National Curriculum 5–16*, July 1987.
15. Ibid, para. 7.

16. *The Independent* throughout November 1987.
17. *The National Curriculum*, para. 8(i).
18. Ibid, para. 8(iii).
19. Ackerman, Bruce: op. cit. see especially Chapters 4 and 5.
20. See Charles Bailey, BPP, pp. 44–45 and 226.
21. *The Report of the Committee of Inquiry into the Education of Children from Ethnic Minority Groups* (The Swann Report) (London, HMSO), March 1985, pp. 364 and 324.
22. Morton-Williams, Roma, Finch, Stewart *et al.*: Schools Council Enquiry 1: *Young School Leavers* (London, HMSO), 1968, p. 45.
23. Raven, John (1977) *Education, Values and Society*, p. 91 (London, Lewis).
24. See works cited under note 13.
25. Ratz, Joseph, op. cit., pp. 407–8.
26. Ibid.

7

The Myth of Cultural Relativism

ROGER SCRUTON*

Britain contains many cultures, several of which are likely to be represented in any single classroom: so we are told by the advocates of 'multi-cultural education'. The observation is used as a ground for rejecting the 'anglocentric' curriculum of our parents. In such circumstances, it is argued, we cannot justify the adoption of a curriculum which is wedded, in both form and content, to a single culture. Our curriculum should be either 'multi-cultural' or 'culture-free', so as to offer equal advantages, and equal opportunities, to every child, whatever his social, ethnic, religious and moral background.

What do we mean by 'culture'? In educational debates, the following have all been included as part of 'culture':

(1) Language, including dialect, speech melody, and idiom.
(2) The 'deep' customs and beliefs of religion.
(3) The 'shallow' customs of social intercourse: feasts and ceremonies, manners and courtesies.
(4) Morality, and especially sexual morality.
(5) Popular entertainment, sport and leisure.
(6) 'High' culture, in which aesthetic values are paramount.
(7) 'Political' culture, including a sense of law and justice, and expectations as to the correct way to resolve conflicts.

Only some of those could conceivably be the subject of a 'choice' on the part of the person who learns them, but clearly all *are* learned, and all are of concern to a person who educates children. It cannot be said that Britain is a 'multi-cultural society' in all seven respects. There is a common language, a dominant religion, a settled pattern of social expectations, a shared network of entertainment and sport, a common morality and a common law. Most of those whose ancestral religion is not Christianity belong to another

*Source: From Scruton, R. (1987) The Myth of Cultural Relativism. In F. Palmer (ed.) *Anti-Racism: an assault on Education and Value*, Sherwood Press, Nottingham.

monotheistic cult which grew from Christianity and Judaism. The Bible is a sacred text for most Britons who are believers; and even the unbelievers share, as a rule, the Judaeo-Christian values of the surrounding order. In 'high' culture there is indeed a radical divide within British society—between those who understand it and those who do not: but it is a divide that has always existed.

This is not to minimize the real difference between the child of Moslem, Urdu-speaking parents, and the child of English-speaking Christians. But there are also great similarities between these two children, who are equally different from the morality of Polynesia, the religion of the Incas or the customs of ancient Japan. To some extent the similarity between them is explained by the pressure exercised by law. Polygamy, for example, is forbidden by English law as is *suttee*. The caste system is legally ineffective and any attempt to act upon it is tortious, if not criminal. Divorce is permitted, and is also a matter for the civil courts. There is freedom of religion, of speech, of opinion. In these and other respects our law exercises a powerful homogenising force, and in no sphere is law more effective than in the sphere of education. For the law, rightly or wrongly, compels people to send their children to school; and if parents cannot afford private schools, the children must perforce mix with those who are gathered into the same classroom as themselves.

It is partly because people overlook the power of the *political* culture of Britain that they imagine such vast differences between the various ethnic groups. If it were the case that one group lived by the caste system, practised polygamy, *suttee* and the stoning to death of adulterers, then it might seriously be suggested that there are vast cultural differences among British citizens. Perhaps a true 'multi-culturalist' would seek to undo the laws which prevent that way of life so that another 'valid alternative' might flourish. As things stand, however, the differences are less significant than the similarities, and the pressure to conformity is enormous. Only in certain crucial matters concerning religious observance are there grounds for thinking that teachers *must* be presented with a problem by their attempts to teach according to the 'anglocentric' curriculum.

That, however, is not the way that the matter is seen by the 'multi-culturalists'. The fact that the teacher can make do with the anglocentric curriculum does not mean that he *ought* to make do with it. For one thing, it is argued, the anglocentric curriculum discriminates against children whose mother tongue is not English. So great is the aversion to 'discrimination' that educationalists argue that children ought to be taught in their mother-tongue, *even though* the surrounding social order is impervious to its utterances. The disastrous consequences of such a policy should be obvious. Deprived of their only opportunity to learn the language of the public world which surrounds them, the children would be destined for a life of social and cultural isolation, in ghettoes, cut off from the larger world and hostile to its law and politics. Of course, there are advocates of 'multi-cultural education' who desire that result, but their disposition to use the ethnic minorities as pawns in the political game of revolution is hardly likely to be shared by the normal British teacher.

No educational process can avoid imparting some culture to those who participate in it. It is impossible to teach children without also teaching them language, good manners, polite and peaceful behaviour and the elements of morality. Without those precious attributes, children could not stay peacefully together in a classroom, nor could they listen to a teacher. It follows that every genuinely educational process must recognize certain cultural expectations as legitimate, and endeavour to support them.

Why, however, do we group together those seven types of activity under the single word 'culture'? All the activities mentioned have this in common: that they serve to bind people together in a common enterprise. To put it another way, they are ways of 'belonging' to the large world of human society, and of affirming one's reality as a social being. Unless people acquire the habit of 'belonging' they cannot live peacefully together, nor can they be happy. Not all ways of belonging have the same structure. The rehearsal of our shared nature in ritual, ceremony and faith is more profoundly rooted than the patient resolution of conflict through law, and the educated obedience to a civil order. The bond which comes from a common religion sincerely believed, and from a solemn enactment of the identity of the tribe, is stronger, more immediate, more overwhelming than the feeling for law. Hence people often look with admiration and nostalgia upon the organic communities in which law is undeveloped, and in which ritual and ceremony carry the principal burden of social existence. Our culture is not—primarily—dependent upon the organic bonds of religion and ceremony. It tries to accommodate conflict and to forge bonds between people by means of contract, law and a shared sense of justice. Indeed, it is frequently argued that this is precisely what distinguishes the modern from the medieval state. The modern state has emerged from that 'prophetic' order, in which people are united behind a revelation of transcendent truth, embodied in ritual and ceremony, to become a 'civil society', in which various religions, various customs and various tastes may co-exist beneath a common rule of law. Many of the philosophers of the European state—Spinoza in particular—advocated just such a transition, believing that the cohesive force of religion is also a source of violent confrontation. Hence, Spinoza argued, religion must be displaced from the centre of political life, and the secular sovereign must be given (through the law) the principal power to administer justice, to uphold association and to establish a common code of conduct. Large questions of political philosophy and sociology are raised by those thoughts. But we can at least see that the *law* of England, and the parliamentary procedure through which it is developed and enacted, are as much parts of the public culture of Britain as is the Christian religion. Any attempt to impart British culture to the children (or grandchildren) of immigrants quite reasonably involves an instruction in the nature of, and the feeling for, the English law: in the *Rechtsgefühl* (the feeling for law and justice) of England, upon which the 'English peace' is ultimately founded.

'British culture' includes any activity, under our seven headings, which facilitates the participation of the individual in the peculiar social order which is Britain. It therefore involves the English language, and the literature that gives to that language its field of reference and its principal communicative power. It also involves the customs and leisure activities that are common to the British people, and—muted though they may be in their consciousness—the religion and history which have given to the law of England its particular force and application.

It is surely a prime duty of a teacher of British children to prepare them for their acceptance into this culture. This does not mean that he must induce a blind obedience to surrounding imperatives or an uncritical acceptance of the myths and dogmas whereby other people live. It means only that, in the end, he will have failed in his duty if the children within his care find that they do not, as a result of their schooling 'belong' to the surrounding world. For to what other world can they turn for the consolations of society? If their education alienates them from the only world to which they have access, what value does it have for them, and why should we compel them to undergo it?

The answer that is often given to those questions is this: British culture is a tawdry and disheartening affair. We should prepare children to free themselves from its grip, not to feel bound by the manacles of history, not to be tied to a particular culture that has outlived its usefulness. But this gives no real argument for rejecting British culture. A child is not free from the grip of a culture simply by being *alienated* from it. On the contrary, alienation is merely a particularly painful form of attachment. Freedom from British culture can be induced only by inducing a state of culture-lessness, or by attaching the child to *another* culture, which is not that of his surrounding world. Neither of those are feasible projects. To void a child's mind of culture is to leave him isolated from fellowship, without the possibility of social fulfilment. If that is what education is supposed to do, then we should all fight to the death against education. To attach a child to another culture, on the other hand, supposes that the teacher himself possesses that culture, and also that he is able to provide the environment that will enable it to thrive. Neither assumption is reasonable, and both lead one to ask why a teacher should really bother with this exercise. Our ancestors did their best to teach their pupils about other cultures: about the culture of Greece and Rome, and that of early Palestine. But they did this in full consciousness that these cultures were extinguished. Hence their teachings were not, in any real sense, a method for presenting children with an existential choice. The attempt to present a genuine *choice* between cultures, to say to the child, this is *one* way of living, this *another*, and now you choose, to do this would require skills, understanding and moral courage beyond the normal or desirable level to which our teachers can aspire.

To transmit the *particular* culture of Britain to the children of Britain is not simply to indoctrinate them in beliefs and values which they are not to question. Almost all cultures contain a principle of internal criticism. It is permissible to question beliefs, even to question values, provided this activity of questioning is contained within the recognized limits of cultural stability. This is particularly true of those cultures—the European—which are founded upon *Rechtsgefühl* as their dominant social perception. The child brought up in the British way of doing things is encouraged to question and to criticize, to seek fair play and impartial judgement, and to receive as doctrine only that which he has independent reason to believe to be true. A child brought up in such a culture does not *need* that presentation of 'alternatives' which so many educationists wish to foist on him. Nor is this openness to question and to other experiences a feature only of our modern culture. Any reader of Shakespeare will recognize the ease with which the poet enters into situations and cultures which are totally outside the ordinary experience of contemporary Englishmen. (Consider Othello, Shylock's daughter, Hamlet, Caliban, Brutus, Cleopatra, Troilus—and a hundred more.)

Advocates of the thesis of cultural relativism often argue as though no culture can really be criticized except from a point of view internal to itself, so that anybody who attempts to judge another culture—a culture with which he does not identify—would be engaged in argument that is without foundation. This thesis, if true, would make the whole idea of a 'choice' of culture absurd: since each culture is insulated from external criticism, there could not conceivably be any reason for choosing between them. However, this kind of relativism is unacceptable. A culture is a pattern of social unity, and can be judged as such; it can be praised or condemned on account of the society that it engenders, and the actual unity which it founds. A culture which holds people together in a state of fear, or which brutally extirpates the natural inclinations of those who share in it, is surely inferior to one that permits peaceful and open dialogue. Nobody would argue that Nazi culture, for example, or Communist culture, are really unjudgeable from any point of view except the one that they themselves define.

This is not to say that there is some *particular* culture that is superior to all others, or that we could establish any canon for evaluating the cultures of other peoples. It is only to say that the very enterprise of social existence is answerable to absolutes of right and wrong. The moral law is universally valid and universally binding; anybody who fails to receive it as such is without morality. A culture that forbids or distorts the truths of morality is objectively undesirable. Of course, it is a difficult philosophical question how we might *justify* the laws of morality. But *what* they are, and *that* they are—these are given to us unquestionably. One of the most important functions of a culture is to rehearse and to support the dictates of morality—to embody them in laws, legends, ceremonies and manners, and so to make them inviolable. Morality therefore provides us with the Archimedean point from which cultures may be weighed, and unless morality too is 'relative'—a view which no one really believes in his actual dealings with his fellows—cultural relativism is false.

That said, we have not yet justified the teaching of *British* culture: all we have done is to propose a test which all cultures must meet if we are to regard them favourably—a test which is met, by and large, by the major cultures of Christendom, Judaism and Islam. Nevertheless, there is already contained in what I have said an intrinsic justification of the British curriculum—and this on two counts:

(1) Children have a prior interest in acquiring the prevailing culture of their surroundings. If they do not acquire it, then their strangeness becomes apparent, and they themselves become victims of discrimination, unable to secure the full advantages of social existence. Hence British children have a prior interest in acquiring British culture.

(2) British culture is a prime example of secular culture, sustained, it is true, by the religious traditions and institutions of Christianity, but based more in open communication and the feeling for law than in any slavish adherence to custom. As an 'open' culture it is manifestly permeable to outside influence, and therefore able to adjust itself to the demands of other customs. (Consider the rapidity with which British language, cooking and costume were penetrated by the language, cooking and costume of India.) Such a culture prepares children for the mobile, mixed society to which they are destined far more effectively than does, for example, the culture of modern Pakistan.

As I have already indicated, this openness of British culture is a long-established feature. One of the reasons for teaching the *high* culture of any society is that it shows this openness at its most developed. A high culture is a sphere of maximum influence, of maximum exposure to what is strange and interesting, of maximum alertness to the human in all its forms: it is the ultimate expression of man's sympathy for his kind. To understand the high culture of Britain is to understand its links with the high cultures of France, Holland, Germany and Spain; with the dead cultures of Greece, Rome and Egypt; with the cultures of Arabia and Persia, and even with those of China and Japan. It is no accident that our culture has reached out to so many others, or provided those cultures with new forms and styles. (To take a few random examples: consider the mutual influence of English and Arabian culture, through such adventurous personalities as Sir Richard Burton; of English and Indian culture through Rudyard Kipling; of English and

Balinese music through Benjamin Britten.) This, indeed, is one of the major justifications that could be offered for what has been called a 'liberal' education, but which might just as well be called an education in the high culture of our civilization.

In the light of those considerations, it seems to me that there can be no real argument for a 'multi-cultural' curriculum. To adopt such a curriculum is to fail to transmit either the common culture of Britain or the high culture that has grown from it. And no other culture is put in the place of those: the result is nothing more than a void, existing in the child's consciousness at precisely the place where certainty, immediacy and competence is needed if he is to engage spontaneously and peacefully within his surrounding world. Teachers have a duty to place their pupils within the broad context of British culture, and, where possible, to foster the development of those wider and more enquiring sympathies that are the substance of a liberal education.

What does this mean in practice? It seems that teaching in our schools ought always to be in English, even if children are encouraged to retain and to develop the mother-tongue which informs their first experience of the world. And the first concern of the history teacher must to be teach the history of Britain, so that a child may understand the past in terms of its present and observable residue. To teach the history of distant and unknown places is, of course, a splendid educational exercise—and one which has always been conducted, under the guise of 'ancient history'. But it cannot substitute for that informed awareness of history as a living process, a form of communication with the past and the future, which stems from an awareness of the 'pastness' of everything one touches, and of the evolving nature of existing society and political arrangements.

Those are only two suggestions, but they point the way to many more. Once the myth of cultural relativism is rejected, we can surely see the way to an improved curriculum, which will be both British in its cultural background and also open to the world, permeable to experience and sympathetic to languages, customs and religions which are not those of modern England.

Part 3

Critiques of Policies

8

Conservative Modernization

KEN JONES*

Conservatism in education—as elsewhere—is three-headed, rather than double-faced. The point can be made in this way: the tendency of free market thought, supported in practice by cultural rightists like Scruton, is to insist that the future of the British economy is dependent almost entirely upon free enterprise and privatization—economic planning of any sort would play little part. It is from this perspective that the Adam Smith Institute approaches education. But in this attitude free market thinkers and traditionalists stand at some distance from a third important aspect of Conservatism, that could roughly be described as a modernizing tendency— not because it is the only current which wishes to achieve economic regeneration and modernizing change in education, but because more deliberately than any other it seeks to intervene in many areas of social life with the prime and specific intention of achieving them. This does not mean that it wishes to return to an economic and political strategy of corporatism: it is intent, rather, on creating an 'enterprise economy' and on reducing union influence, and thus borrows much from the free market programme. It does, however, intend that the pace and the content of change should be shaped by state intervention. In education this entails the belief that the content of the curriculum is far too important to be left to the autonomy of the individual school. The free marketeers and the cultural right may see the state's role as essentially negative, in putting down all those forces— bureaucratic or insurgent—which in Scruton's words 'threaten ancient shackles which now chain down the potential for economic and for individual development'. Thus, while no opponent of selection, the modernizing tendency has no time for the grammar school tradition. Unlike the cultural right, it considers it to be part of the problem, not the solution. It is thoroughly critical of the anti-industrial values of a liberal education: the state schools of the present century have reproduced many of the failings of

*Source: From Jones, K. (1989) *Right Turn: The Conservative Revolution in Education*, Hutchinson Radius, London.

the public schools that some of them have tried to emulate, and have preserved a rigid distinction between high-status academic knowledge and low-status practical training. Adhering to a book-bound curriculum, they offer to students an education which many find irrelevant and demotivating. The modernizers, by contrast, present their programme as a means not only of serving industry but—by knocking down the academic/practical barrier—of democratizing knowledge, and of enabling students to demonstrate kinds of achievement which the old education neither fostered nor recognized.

This, though, is only half the burden of the modernizers' arguments. For them, state education combines the worst of the old with the worst of the reforming new. The shackles they want to throw off are not only those forged by a nineteenth-century intelligentsia. It is because of the character and direction of *modern* state education that the school has become what one compilation of industrialists' views calls 'an adventure playground for educationalists', in which a 'laudable compassion for disadvantaged pupils may have produced a "softness" which is markedly at variance with the competitive requirements of industry'. Thanks to a school culture that combines lukewarm attitudes to science with an anti-industrial bias, 'many young people [are] more interested in courses which they feel would help them reform and heal society' than in becoming technologists and engineers. Alongside the 'democratic' claims of the modernizers runs a determination to put an end to these more malign effects of progressive reform, and to establish at the heart of education new kinds of attitude and purpose.

It is a project that needs to be seen against a wider background, a vaster educational process that runs through the capillaries of British society: a general Conservative effort, expressed in many different areas of policy, to re-educate the population, whether as workers or as citizens. This process has many strands, most of which converge on a single, broad and unifying theme: the fostering of a mentality that looks to individual initiative as the prime means of advance, and that forsakes belief in collective action either by trade unionists or a politically active citizenry. The hammer blows directed against trade unions, the centralization of political life and the authoritarianism of much social policy are one side of this process. The other is the enlargement of consumer freedoms and market influence which goes with every new measure of privatization and deregulation. Translated into terms of 'initiative' and 'enterprise'—and interwoven with the concerns introduced by the cultural right—this form of re-education runs through the entire programme for modernizing the school.

Yet remarkably this project has proved attractive to many of those associated with education reform, who have accepted elements of its diagnosis and welcomed much of what it says about curriculum change, even while they have dissented from and tried to modify other parts of its programme. They give modernization this reception because it draws its criticisms and prescriptions from a repertoire which, historically, has been more the property of reforming tendencies than of thinkers of the Black Paper variety. Its demand, for instance, that schools should encourage other kinds of achievement than the academic is one that has been made widely by reformers. Its preference for experience-based learning likewise echoes reforming traditions, and its comments on the irrelevance of education to the lives of many students also strikes a familiar note. Of course, there is much suspicion about the general purposes of the modernizers' programme of change, but, on the whole, it is one that can be worked with. Its concerns, unlike those of the right, do not to seek a confrontation with reform at the everyday level of classroom working. Indeed, in some respects, the modernizers appear to base their changes on the best of current, progressive-influenced practice.

The following sections try first of all to understand this *rapprochement*: to explain why modernization makes use of some progressive themes and what it does to alter them.

[. . .].

Progressivism was held responsible by the right for many of the ills of education. Allegedly, it downplayed the importance of the factual basis of learning, created social relations in the classroom that prevented learning, and, by stressing the sacrosanct needs of the child, neglected the importance of transmitting the essential principles of the national culture. Above all, perhaps, it sacrificed quality for equality: by insisting on equal treatment for all children, it diverted attention from the needs of elite groups. Certainly, these complaints were right to identify something radical in progressivism. Despite its diverseness, it can still be termed a modernizing tendency of a broadly left-wing kind. In the 1920s—its classical period—it had been critical of 'industrial society' and social authoritarianism. As taken up in the 1960s by promoters of reform, it added to these commitments a concern to eradicate educational disadvantage. From the early part of the century right through to the 1970s, 'progressivism', taking its stand on the need of students fully to express their potential, had counterposed its views to the requirements of an economic system which was run on quite different principles. As one progressive headteacher put it in 1976:

> If our objective is to assist the students to take increasing control of their own destinies, to question assumptions, to solve problems by being inventive and trained to envisage speculative alternatives, we are bound to meet conflict with an industrial society that sees schools principally as the sorting house for employment.

How, then, with this record of critique, could elements of progressivism be incorporated into a new vocationalist orthodoxy? The most convincing answer is that for a long period it was the only tendency to address curricular and pedagogic questions basic to the efficiency of a mass education system in a developed capitalist society. Any such system will need ideas for securing students' motivation to learn, and thus for devising curricula that are relevant to their lives. Any such society will need from its work-force and citizens a range of skills and qualities that cannot be developed within the bounds of an academic schooling. These are among the reasons for progressivism's attractiveness to educational policy-makers—an attractiveness that has lasted several decades, and is not likely to be dispelled by the critiques of a new right which does not even recognize the existence of the problems the progressives address.

[. . .]

The primary school, in the 1960s, was the main focus and generator of influential models of education. In the era of Baker and Joseph—of training for responsible citizenship and the world of work—the emphasis has shifted to the secondary years. Here selfhood has now a very different language. 'For us', Kenneth Baker told his party conference in 1986, 'education must fulfil the individual's potential, not stifle it in the name of egalitarianism'. White Papers demand a 'climate in which people can be motivated and their creative capacity harnessed'. Businessmen complain that education 'diminishes the life chances and inhibits the talents of many people'. The new education, with equal opportunity at its heart, will ensure that 'the achievements of all, whatever their race, sex or class, can be raised'. The language is excited, promise-crammed, attentive to individual need.

But what, on second hearing, is the meaning of the terms—'individual', 'creative' and so on—with which the discourse is saturated? How much do they overlap with, or abandon, the meanings of Plowden? 'Creative' by now is fairly familiar: it relates to entrepreneurial endeavour, rather than to the imaginative qualities which it *used* to denote. 'Individual' is used in a more complex way. In part, it validates inequality—the needs of the individual requiring increased distinction between the kinds of education available to students of different abilities. But it also suggests the kinds of learner whom education is addressing—both the personal qualities he or she already possesses, and those the school should be producing in them. In this sense it is very revealing of the ideas of culture and of human development that underlie the modernizing aspects of the Conservative programme.

Its conception of the individual is, in cultural terms, a very abstract one. Conservatives of the Scruton kind write about *belonging*; for them, individuals are constituted by the culture they live in, and the tasks of politics relate to maintaining the cohesion of that culture. It is from this angle that they view history, literature, leisure and all the transactions of everyday life. All are given a significance, that links in one direction with the nature of individuality, and in the other with the political order. Baker himself is happy on occasion to toy with views like these. No minister is more fulsome in evoking images of an idyllic Englishness, product of 'a unique and beautiful country', or in praising the English language, 'our mother tongue . . . our greatest asset as a nation . . . the essential ingredient of the Englishness of England'; nor more immersed in an imperial imagination, whether he is evoking the 'fever trees of the Limpopo', or the 'teeming presence of India'.

Baker is concerned, albeit gesturally, with the cultural medium through which individuality is lived. The themes of the modernizing tendency, on the other hand, are in an important sense acultural. 'Belonging', 'community' and the problems of social solidarity are not at its centre, and its conception of the individual is correspondingly non-concrete. It quietly assumes the unproblematic existence of a unified national culture, but lacks the urgent assertiveness of the right that such a culture must be transmitted to all social groups. Thus, questions of culture operate more as an implicit background to modernization than as immediate, strongly-argued themes.

Despite the problems that it has with the concept of individuality, in other ways the new education seeks to shape and monitor personal development more attentively than ever before. Though the cultural aspects of the individual are scarcely glimpsed, the qualities required by the world of work are put in much more concrete terms. The report on *Competence and Competition* puts the issue most clearly, in identifying a difference between the aims of education as previously accepted in Britain, and those promoted in other countries, which 'consciously' include 'such training objectives as teamwork, flexibility and the desire to learn'. In Britain, the tendency has been to regard them as 'personal qualities' rather than vocational outcomes. Qualities which have previously been considered 'personal'—in the sense that Plowden's conceptions were 'personal'—should be relocated in a different context, with a highly pronounced vocational stress. On the 'desire to learn', for instance, the report notes that:

> the difficulty is not that people do not want to learn. Britain has one of the most highly developed adult education systems in the world. The success of the Open University is just one of the many indications that the desire to learn continues. The WEA still has 170,000 members. . . . What seems to have happened is that people want to learn but they perceive that learning to be related to their private interests or to matters which make them more independent of their employers.

This has to change. Desire for knowledge and satisfaction with learning must be transferred to the area of 'competent performance' in employment. Human development is to be relocated in occupational training.

Nor is this a change only at the level of statements of intent. A pedagogy has arisen that pays the most detailed attention to means by which a new sense of self can be inculcated in working-class students, by means of what Phillip Cohen has called a 'micro-technology of self-improvement'. The 'Social and Life Skills' courses that are now widespread in schools and colleges teach 'techniques of impression management designed to help students project a positive self-image to employers'. In doing so, they disparage the cultures of home and street as obstacles to successful employment and encourage 'the crassest and most individualist strategies of adaptation to mass unemployment.' In this sense, it is possible to speak of the 'new person' that modernized education means to create: eager to adapt, convinced of the rewards of individual enterprise, accepting and enacting the values of the business climate around them.

There is a problem, however, with a stress like this. Conservative ideologists themselves are aware that an educational—as well as a wider cultural—hegemony requires a broader base than vocationalism can provide. Conservative Britain proliferates with schemes for the creation of work-orientated personalities, and its leaders are skilful with a rhetoric of standards and excellence. They are not so comfortable with those aspects of culture which establish a regime's claim to a higher legitimacy, as a guardian angel of creativity. In a speech on the teaching of English in late 1986, Baker, with an eye on credentials of this kind, insisted that 'the new and proper emphasis on the application and practical aspects of subjects . . . should not lead to any diminution in the magic and potency of literature'. In his earlier incarnation as chair of the MSC, Lord Young pleaded with an audience, 'I hope you will not consider me a philistine. . . . I recognize the need for artistic endeavour, for the enhancement of our cultural life, for a need to give us all the interest and the interests to spend our ever-increasing leisure.' Both men, aware that reference to 'employers' needs' would not on this occasion clinch the argument, looked elsewhere, outside the world of work, to discover qualities that contribute to the education of the whole person. But rather than presenting with modernist enthusiasm the qualities that a new education could develop in students, they fell back on the rhetorical conventions of a not-very-recent past, which are quite unable to address the cultural experience of the late twentieth century. Baker's invocation of the 'magic of literature' is a weary trope, that places literature outside social life. It belongs, like many of his cultural reference points to an antiquated literary tradition. The paradox is striking. His government has fostered one of the great modern attempts to transform ideas and sensibilities. In all its efforts the role of the media has been crucial, in building up the great demons and desires of popular culture in the Thatcher era. By the mid-1990s, television and radio will have been subjected to increasingly direct commercial influence. The dominance of purely financial criteria for programme-making will lead to the same downmarket spiralling as that which has taken the tabloid press to new depths. Yet Baker, a leading member of a Cabinet which has set all this in motion, speaks warily of the 'marshy ground' of 'modern culture' and appeals to the magic of literature against a TV culture 'much of which is mundane and brain-numbing'. This disparity, between a traditionalist idea of culture, set out in its Sunday best on ministerial speech days, and the cultural activities more usually associated with Thatcherism, indicates something incomplete and—even in its own terms—unsatisfactory about the Conservative programme. In the Jekyll and Hyde *mélange* which is the rhetoric of Kenneth Baker, the Jekyll-Baker of cultural tradition steps back in horror from the Baker-Hyde of 'commercialization'. Yet both, of course, are aspects of Conservatism. It is as if it dare not cultivate in schools the intellectual qualities to understand the processes and sensibilities which it has been largely responsible for creating.

The strongest restrictions, however, on the development of the individual are those that arise from the anti-democratic nature of the Conservative programme, and from its fervent commitment to inequality. Every routine reference made by curriculum documents to an education that will 'enable people to participate effectively in a democracy' is offset by some practical measure that inhibits discussion of a controversial issue, or that curtails the exercise of democratic right. Likewise, for every claim that the ERA opens opportunities, there is some new step in social policy that actively deprives the most disadvantaged people of the means which would enable their families to benefit from, or continue with, their education. So although the national curriculum is glowingly presented as an *entitlement* curriculum for all students, in practice there are many restrictions on such entitlement. The under-resourcing of education is the most evident, but for particular groups there are others equally disabling. At national level, there are no inducements for students from poor families to remain in education after 16: financially, they would be better off if they took a place on the Youth Training Scheme. The unemployed parents of school-age children will not find it possible, on an 1988 weekly income of about £70, to be able to meet the school's increasing requests for parental contributions, nor to provide the investment of time and energy that the slogan of parent empowerment demands. The obvious in these times needs restating: poverty is a great disenfranchiser; gross inequality cannot be the basis for democracy in education, nor for the development of an individual's potential.

Yet restrictions of this sort have not prevented 'democracy' and 'equal opportunity' from becoming central claims in the Conservative rhetoric of education. The basis of such a claim is set out in its most coherent form by Lord Young, who outlines the theories of knowledge that underpin the new education. Here, too, the weaknesses of the modernizers' case demands attention.

Modern Knowledge

In May 1984 David Young, head of the MSC and prime mover of TVEI was three months away from ennoblement and Cabinet status. In that month, he gave the Haldane Memorial Lecture at Birkbeck College—*Knowing How and Knowing That: A Philosophy of the Vocational*. Education, he begins his lecture, 'has concentrated upon academic and intellectual pursuits to the detriment of the practical'. Academic education is based on 'intellectual operations'; it is 'primarily deductive'. Borrowing a term from the philosopher Gilbert Ryle, of whom he is apparently a follower, Young calls it 'knowing that'. He counterposes this kind of knowledge to 'knowing how'—'intelligent practice', that embodies a knowledge that cannot be translated into the language of the intellect, and cannot be derived from it. The skier, the painter, the plumber and the entrepreneur all provide examples of 'knowing how'. Education under-values it, and thus has a narrow conception of what constitutes intelligence. Young would widen the concept, to include not only qualities of artistic intelligence, but also those of being 'good at problem solving', 'highly practical', and 'good with one's hands'. Intrinsically, these are just as valid and important and desirable as knowing that. Young suggests, in fact, that on occasion they are more desirable. 'I sometimes dream', he confides, 'that if we lived in a world in which there was no Oxbridge and the highest form of academic establishment was the Slade School of Art, we would have different values. In that world we might well think of a painter as "educated", even those who could draw or make things as able, and give scant consideration to those who could merely grasp academic concepts.'

Young, though, is not merely concerned with reordering the hierarchies of knowledge. His argument has a direct economic application. Democratiz-ing knowledge is the key to modernization and competitiveness. The academic tradition in education was one of the reasons why, in the late nineteenth century, 'we lost our competitive edge'. Now, 'the gust of social change' makes it even more imperative that we have 'a working population both educated and trained, not just in the academic, the pure or the theoretical, but one with broadly based skills, able to adapt to change'. These skills will embrace several qualities—above all entrepreneurial ones. Large-scale industry is a thing of the past for Britain. Foreigners can do it more cheaply and more effectively. What is needed instead is 'a host of small companies, companies that will provide services . . . companies that will depend for their very existence on entrepreneurial skills, rapid development of products, customer service and a pragmatic and practical approach to life'.

This is the future, in which the development of the all-round personality and of the economy are perfectly synchronized. Towards the end of his talk, in a kind of visionary coda, Young attempts to draw together his philosophical and his economic themes. The labour market of the future will require schools to produce 'whole people', who will avoid narrow specialisms and will be prepared 'for a world as yet unknown'. Their knowledge will not be narrowly academic. They will know how the democratic system works. They will know what private industry is about, and the 'importance, place and use of profits'. They will be able 'to fix washers on taps'; to 'prepare and paint a door'; to use 'a keyboard, a library or an electric drill'. Above all, rounding their personalities and attainments, they will be equipped with the lingua franca and the open sesame of the modern world. For, says Young, in an analogy which could serve as a memorial to the breadth and humanity of his vision, just as 'Latin was vital to the educated of the fourteenth century, so a knowledge of taxation and marketing is to the educated of the twenty-first century'.

Much can be said about the relation of Young's philosophy to his policies: between the theory of knowledge that he holds and the way it relates to the social order whose transformations he observes. First are the problems inherent in the sharpness of his distinction between 'knowing how' and 'knowing that'. Young imagines that the activity of an artist or a footballer is spontaneous and unreflective. It cannot be taught, and the principles which guide it cannot be fully expressed. When a footballer passes the ball, 'he just passes it there'. There is no time for concept formation: 'the thought is the action'. When an institute tries to teach aesthetic 'taste'—as in matters of town planning—environmental disaster follows. These propositions are dubious. In fact, within any 'knowing how' there is a 'knowing that', which can include—in the case of an athlete or a painter—a learned knowledge of technique, elements of deductive thinking, and a knowledge about the context of the activity. Each of these qualities is capable of being taught. A footballer can know from coaching and by deduction where the ball should go; a skier will need knowledge about weather conditions, and so on. The general point is that no activity, however 'practical', is as unreflective, as devoid of conceptual thinking, as Young would like to make it. As the psychologist Vygotsky put it, all 'higher psychic functions', whose main features are reflection, awareness and deliberate control, are dependent not on motor reflexes, but on conceptual development, which in turn involves a development of language: 'signs are the basic means used to master and control them'. Young's expulsion of the conceptual from practical activity has particular, ultimately political, consequences.

Equally questionable are the issues that arise from his claim that, 'Knowing how is just as valid a form of intelligence as knowing that'. The historic downgrading of the first in favour of the second is not just a matter of prejudices of intellectuals. Elite education gave preference to intellectual skills, including those of developed abstract thought, because they are essential to understanding and controlling natural and social forces. Countries and businesses are not run by those who possess practical intelligence alone. It is superficially democratic to preach the equivalence of the practical with the abstract—it seems to offer the possessors of practical skills equality with those trained in abstract thought. In reality, the argument serves to crystallize existing social differences, by suggesting that there is no great need for those excluded by history and education from access to the linguistic tools of thought to make an effort to acquire them. And this is the stress of Young's argument: not to integrate 'practical' elements with an 'academic' education, but continually to suggest that a 'valid' education can be constructed around the principles of 'knowing how'. Antonio Gramsci, observing the practical turn of Italian mass education in the 1920s, understood the falsity of a prospectus like Young's.

He criticized schools which were designed 'to satisfy immediate, practical interests', and noted behind their egalitarian, democratic watchwords a refusal to develop in students the capacity 'to reason, to think abstractedly and schematically while remaining able to plunge back from abstraction into real and immediate life, to see in each fact or datum what is general and what is particular, to distinguish the concept from the specific instance'. This refusal of the school, matched now by the direction of Young's argument, left access to the skills of reasoning open only to the already dominant social groups.

In Young's thought, the so-called 'practical' (which in fact comprises the typical mental activity of millions of people) is severed in the sharpest of ways from the intellectual. This is especially significant in view of the way that he connects the narrowly-defined practical to the 'world of work', in such a way as to prevent 'abstract and schematic thought' from being brought to bear upon it. When John Dewey, most profound of progressive thinkers, argued for vocational education, he saw it as an activity which 'acknowledges the full intellectual and social meaning of a vocation', including 'instruction in the historic background of present conditions; training in science to give intelligence and initiative in dealing with material and agencies of production; and study of economics, civics and politics to bring the future worker into touch with the problems of the day and the various methods proposed for their improvement'. Politics, ethics and history were not extraneous to Dewey's concept of education, but integral to it. This is not the case with Young. In the appalling innocence of his claim that taxation and marketing are core aspects of a new renaissance in education, he lacks any serious consideration of the way industrial and commercial activities relate to human need. Thus the kind of change that Young advocates is far from being a democratization of school knowledge. In essence it endorses a narrowed concentration on the practical tasks involved in 'knowing how', at the expense of the issues which examination of the work process from a wider point of view can reveal.

Education, Enterprise, Equal Opportunities

Young's arguments were not just the personal musings of a man soon to be Cabinet Minister. He was speaking as chair of the MSC, and his words reflected the essentials of its programme for educational change. The MSC, established by a Conservative government and set up in 1974 with full trade union support, had grown in influence during the 1970s. After initial suspicions of its corporate status ministers in Mrs Thatcher's government began to see it as a body with considerable potential. It became part of a general government effort to 'encourage an enterprise economy'. The Department of Employment, in describing its own work, shows how this economy is being constructed. Its first task is to promote the new growth sectors of the economy—such as small firms, self-employment and tourism. The second is to unleash market forces while weakening the power of unions to withstand them—or, as the Department more guardedly puts it, 'to help business grow and jobs to multiply by cutting red tape, improving industrial relations under the law by ensuring a fair balance and encouraging employee involvement'. The third is to 'improve training arrangements'. In the rhetoric of enterprise, these improvements involve providing high levels of skill and competence for all. 'The jobs of the future', says Kenneth Baker, 'will be upmarket jobs'.

An unravelling of the meanings of the Conservative programme can usefully begin with this last claim, that modernization necessitates higher skills and thus a better education for all. This is half the truth. The European TUC describes the major employment trends of the continent's economy as 'the creation of a small number of jobs requiring specialized training and high qualification; the elimination of many jobs on low and intermediate levels of skill; the lowering of skills required in many existing jobs'. The American heart of high technology, Silicon Valley, is itself, according to a journal of the American left, a land of 'two labor forces', as 'different in composition, wages and working conditions as if they belonged to two entirely separate industries'. While electronics engineers enjoy 'programmes and benefits that read like the entries in an encyclopedia of innovative workplace experience', for the production workers who make up half the industry, 'Silicon Valley means low-wage, dead-end jobs, unskilled tedious work and exposure to some of the most dangerous health hazards in all of American industry.' Others have pointed to the way these tendencies affect the British work-force. Against a background of incessant attacks on trade unionism—by law, by redundancy, by the media, by the loosening of health and safety and fair wage provision, by cuts in the social wage, an uneven modernization is taking place. In substantial ways, as miners, engineers, steelworkers have cause to know, it entails deindustrialization: the closure on a huge scale of uncompetitive or unprotected production. In others it involves growth: in the financial sector, and in high technology related industry. In the process, both areas have become more thoroughly integrated into international finance systems and divisions of labour. Around the successful large-scale enterprises, clusters of service and sub-contracting industries develop, some on the basis of self-employment, which increased greatly in and after the recession. This kind of modernization entails radically different experiences for different social groups. The areas of employment growth are, on the one hand, among 'managers, administrators, engineers, scientists and technicians'; and, on the other, in part-time, temporary or casual employment—low-paid work for which women are thought particularly suitable. These latter jobs could be in private services, in the public sector, or on the sub-contracting periphery of manufacturing, where workers can be hired or laid off according to the week-by-week requirements of the market. The demands of employers thus take two major forms. There is both a chronic, unsatisfied need for 'skilled, technical and craft workers', and a demand for casual and part-time employees who can spend the rest of their time on the fringes of the social security state. All sections of the work-force, however, will face a more volatile labour market, in which there is an increased possibility that they will be required to change jobs, develop flexibility, or, especially if they do not belong to the core of the work-force, adapt themselves to periods of unemployment. In a brief and less florid section of his lecture, Young had recognized this. He turned away from his vision of an entrepreneurial future, to make it plain that 'knowing how' has a special meaning for the less successful. 'Many, in our society of tomorrow', he said, 'whether they are true entrepreneurs or not, are going to have to take on responsibility for their own lives and economic welfare—to become more self-sufficient'. Responsibility in these cases involved acceptance of periods of unemployment and of periodic retraining.

It was against this background—of a process of modernization that was selective in its effects, but that was frequently mis-presented by an upmarket rhetoric—that the MSC was encouraged to increase the speed at which it changed from provider of special programmes to combat unemployment, to organizer of universal change in the employment and training of young people. A series of initiatives between 1981 and 1987 accelerated the transformation of the youth labour market and the training institutions associated with it. Jobs for young people virtually dried up. The apprenticeship system went into sharp decline. The 'Industrial Training Boards' which had been able to levy employers in order to fund skill training were for the most part abolished. In their place appeared a proliferation of programmes, at the centre of which were youth schemes of ever-increasing size. These programmes culminated in 1983 in the Youth Training Scheme (YTS)—designed to accommodate all jobless school-leavers. The claim was that YTS would provide a 'bridge between school and work', that linked work experience with training in a range of skills which would not be specific to any one job, but would be transferable across an 'occupational family'. YTS was intended to create a new kind of work-force, one that, in the words of Nigel Lawson, would have the 'right skills' and would be 'adaptable, reliable, motivated and prepared to work at wages that employers can afford to pay'. Sceptics disputed the first of Lawson's claims. Even assuming a two-tier economy, they said, YTS was not delivering either the quantity or the quality of training that regeneration required. The skill shortages which have become apparent in many sectors of the mid-1980s economic recovery bear out these criticisms, and indeed, were one of the reasons that Conservatives gave for winding up the MSC in 1988. Its functions were transferred to a new body, the Training Agency, that was even more clearly employer-led.

Other critics objected to the demands implied in the second part of Lawson's statement, at the same time recognizing their accuracy: the main function of YTS was to keep youth off the streets, while depressing its wages and job expectations. They also scrutinized the content of YTS, as they had done its predecessors. For an insufficient minority, perhaps, who had access to something resembling the old apprenticeship schemes, there would be good quality training. For the most part, however, YTS merely prepared large numbers of people for low-skilled, insecure employment. Its schemes concentrated on the inculcation of appropriate attitudes to work on 'social and communications skills'. One critic termed them 'skills training for deskilling, job preparation for unemployment'. They provided neither craft training, nor recognizable educational achievements, but concentrated on developing such qualities as 'motivation', 'self-esteem' and 'co-operativeness'—as if these nebulous achievements were of use to the trainee in the labour market, or educationally. Yet, for reasons which will by now not be surprising, the new line in training borrowed much from progressive education. The Social and Life Skills courses omnipresent in YTS were supposedly relevant to the everyday concerns of working-class youth, and their experience-based model of learning, that shunned most forms of explicit conceptualization, gained credence, as Andy Green has commented, 'through its apparent appropriateness to those who have demonstrated their aversion to academic teaching in the schools'. YTS, thus, was much more than a training scheme: it generated influential new models of education for a new kind of world of work.

It was on the basis of the growing educational sophistication of MSC programmes that, in 1982, Young had launched a 'Technical and Vocational Education Initiative' at schools. Symbolically, its birth was announced not by the Education Secretary, who appears to have known little about it, but by the Prime Minister. The intention was to subject the school to the shock of outside, vocational influence, that could force the emergence of a new curriculum. The first response of educationists to TVEI was suspicion. They thought it would reinforce divisions in schools between academic and vocational streams; it was an unwelcome, centralizing intruder in a locally-adminstered school system; it would have more to do with job training than with general education.

Opinions soon changed, both because of the money the MSC could offer the selected 'pilot' areas and the progressive curriculum criteria that its National Steering Group devised. The existence of criteria, rather than set syllabuses, diminished fears of centralization, while ensuring a degree of conformity to general, MSC-set principles. They combined progressive with work-oriented themes. They pledged TVEI to developing 'equal opportunities for both sexes'—a commitment that has, as we shall see, been taken with some seriousness. Their learning objectives included, 'the encouraging of initiative, problem-solving abilities and other aspects of personal development'. To avoid one-sidedness, they specified that courses had to have a balance between general, technical and vocational elements, varying according to students' individual needs and the stages of the course, while relating technical and vocational elements to potential employment opportunities. Thus it became clear that TVEI would not be merely a school-based version of YTS: it would be better-funded and broader in its educational content. This shift in emphasis—which became more pronounced as TVEI developed—away from the 'vocational' towards the more educationally-acceptable 'technical' was not the result of some sudden change of heart at the MSC. It was rather the effect of pressure from the educational world, both from the top, among the education authorities which formulated individual schemes, and from the classroom teachers who had the work of devising projects and curricula. TVEI was assimilated within education, in a way that showed something of the detailed process of modernization: though the result of government initiative, it was not a simple imposition upon schools; the themes of the enterprise economy merged with the pre-existing interests of the schools, to form new types of curriculum. Critical assessment of the modernizing tendency must thus take into account not only the origins of the initiative, but also the way it changed at school level. Yet, for all this, it must not lose sight of the relationship between even the most progressive of modernizing schemes, and the overall emphases of the enterprise economy.

Under the scheme, LEAs draw up proposals for school-based projects, in the main aimed at 14–16-year-olds. Those which were approved by the National Steering Group were funded by the MSC and became subject to its regular evaluation. Beginning with 14 'pilot' areas in 1983, the scheme spread quickly. By 1985 74 out of the 104 LEAs in England and Wales were involved. Two years later it had become a 'national' scheme. In the process, it distanced itself from its explicitly vocational origins. By the middle of 1985, Lord Young could give it a new tone. It was 'not just about employable skills', but about 'educating people, about broadening the curriculum to give them new subjects to which to relate'. Within education, as one of its enthusiasts wrote, TVEI had become accepted as 'mainstream curricular reform with a long pedigree'. The educational press found that in several ways it echoed classic progressive practice.

> Young people of all abilities appreciate a more applied and vocational slant to their studies. . . . Many respond well to courses which break the conventional timetable mould, allowing whole days or half-days to be spent on project work or work experience. . . . The practical and technical are as highly valued as the academic. . . . Teacher/learner relationships are improved and changed.

Academic evaluations considered that it was 'eminently liberal and student-centred'. Pupils' responses 'almost without exception were extremely positive and favourable'. Teachers 'weighed in' to ensure that schemes were based on 'the comprehensive principle', with no growth of technical streams and no narrowing of educational experience.

The published syllabuses of local schemes, and the copious documentation the MSC supplies, allow some assessment of how TVEI's general principles worked out in local practice. It is possible to see in this process both the extent to which schools have modified TVEI's initial impetus, and the limits of that modification. Schools have moved away from the severely functional emphases of MSC philosopy while at the same time they have not sought to challenge its fundamental conceptions of the relation of learning to industry. The Hertfordshire scheme was one of the least equivocal about its industrial orientation. Its 'starting point' was an 'assessment of the skills and experience likely to be needed by industry and business locally and nationally'. It was decided that TVEI should include: 'industrial studies: how business functions in all its aspects'; computing and information technology; modern engineering design; electronics; modern office skills; 'an understanding of the manufacturing process from the identification of the need for a product, through its design, prototype, manufacture, testing, packaging and marketing phases'.

The much-studied Devon scheme is more liberal in its starting point. 'All TVEI students cover three areas of learning—technology at work, the world of business, personal and caring services.' Technology at work involves identifying a particular problem, finding and producing a technical solution to it, and evaluating the effectiveness of that solution. In the 'world of business', the technical aspects of production are complemented by study of the social relations it involves. Through first-hand experience—visits, interviews, research—students will come to understand business organization. They will find out about 'personal problems at work by interviewing adult workers about their jobs, by identifying an area of concern either from the management or the workers' point of view, and by investigating the work of the personnel department' and the counselling available to workers. Under the same heading, students will look at the role of finance institutions in relation to firms and individuals, discover the applications of modern technology in working life and 'explain the effects of local industry on the environment and community'. In the final part of the triad, 'the full range of study skills' is employed to learn about 'personal and caring services', that include 'community associations, domestic services, educational provision, facilities for the disabled, housing, recreation, libraries, religious and voluntary organizations', and so on. Alongside these courses are the by now familiar elements of an education for the new kind of individual: 'areas of personal study, such as coping strategies, self-presentation, deportment, grooming, diet, health, hygiene, safety and the use of household equipment'.

TVEI schemes combine, then, an orientation to the world of work with strategies for learning that emphasize relevance, inquiry and the use of modern technology. They make one further claim to progressivism: to be dealing with equal opportunity—especially in relation to gender—in a more radical and systematic way than any other initiative. It is not merely that TVEI incorporates aspects of the pedagogies of reform; it is also that under its aegis reform's objectives can be pursued with a new seriousness. The scheme sponsors a 'networking' of teachers, so that equal opportunity policies are not left as formal commitments, but are popularized and collectively developed. TVEI publications explain this concern in several ways. In philosophical terms, equal opportunity is a 'human right' which education should be promoting. More mundanely, 'in order to halt the decline in international competitiveness, the country needs to be able to harness the talents of all its people to their fullest extent'. There is a need for increased provision of certain types of female labour, some professional or technical, most casual and 'semi-skilled'. After all, most jobs that the economy has gained over the last ten years have been done part time, mainly by women, in areas like, office work, tourism, leisure, catering, and so on.

TVEI's equal opportunity work centres on equality of access for girls to traditionally male subjects and jobs. Access can be made easier if role stereotyping is avoided, if positive role models are provided, and if the self-image of girls is strengthened. Teachers' attitudes have to be changed. Girls' interests must be seen as equal in status to those of boys. Boys themselves need to take seriously the conventional female areas of responsibility for families and parenthood. Outside the school, there must be a revaluation of the work women do. 'Only when women's jobs and qualities are valued equally with men's' will the character of life and learning change so as to make equal opportunities a vital principle.

If the principles of TVEI-in-practice are seriously to be challenged, it should be at this strong and provocative point of the scheme, where Conservative initiatives seem to have stimulated progressive methods and equal opportunity policies. Is it really the case that TVEI curricula give girls a fuller understanding of the part of work in their lives, and in this way empower them to press for change? Or is it rather that TVEI is still in essence a scheme trapped within the categories of Young's lecture, incapable of developing what Gramsci called 'abstract and schematic thinking', and of fulfilling the task that Dewey imposed on education, of 'bringing the future worker into touch with the problems of the day and the various methods proposed for their improvement'?

TVEI is in many respects an advance on the traditional curriculum. But, it still does not deliver, in any full and adequate sense, the kind of education that Dewey envisaged.

References

1. See, for example Anderson, D. (ed.) (1984) *Trespassing : Businessmen's views on the Education System*, Social Affairs Unit and David Young's Haldane Memorial Centre: *Knowing How and Knowing That : A Philosophy of the Vocational*, published by Birkbeck College, London in 1984.

2. Ranson, S., Taylor, B. and Brighouse, T. (1986) The Revolution in Education and Training.
3. Watts, J. Headteacher of Countesthorpe College in Fletcher, C. *et al.* (1985) *Schools on Trial: the trials of democratic comprehensives.*
4. Manpower Services Commission (M.S.C.) (1984) Competence and Competition, London, HMSO.

9

The New Right and the National Curriculum: state control or market forces?[1]

GEOFF WHITTY*

This paper takes as its starting point an apparent tension within the Education Reform Act between its imposition of a national curriculum and its stress elsewhere on parental choice and market forces in determining the shape of the school system. The paper then explores differences within the New Right over the issue of the school curriculum, but also points to ways in which neo-liberal and neo-conservative positions may ultimately be reconcilable. However, it also suggests that neither position may prove entirely attractive to the government's industrial sponsors who wish the curriculum to be more responsive to the needs of industry. The paper then draws on the findings of a recent research project on school choice to consider some possible consequences of allowing market forces to determine the nature of the curriculum. In conclusion, it stresses the importance of seeing the national curriculum within its broader structural context and notes that there are important lessons to be drawn from the approaches taken by both the tendencies identified within New Right thinking about the curriculum.

> I sometimes think that a study of the life and teachings of Adam Smith should be compulsory in all schools. Bob Dunn addressing the IEA in July 1988 (quoted in *Education*, 8 July 1988).

In one of the many consultation papers issued during the passage of the Education Reform Bill, the government asserted that it was 'taking action to increase the autonomy of schools and their responsiveness to parental wishes' (DES, 1987). The provisions in the Education Reform Act on open

*Source: From Whitty, G. (1989) The New Right and the National Curriculum: State control or market forces? *Journal of Educational Policy* Vol. 4, No. 4, pp. 329–341.

enrolment, financial delegation, grant maintained schools and city technology colleges were all presented by the government as consistent with this aim. They were presented as building upon the parental choice and accountability provisions of the 1980 Education Act and, more particularly, those of the 1986 Education (No. 2) Act, which enhanced the powers of the governors and increased the influence on governing bodies of parents and members of the local business community. The government claimed, for example, that grant maintained schools would 'add a new and powerful dimension to the ability of parents to exercise choice within the publicly provided sector of education' and that 'parents and local communities (would) have new opportunities to secure the development of their schools in ways appropriate to the needs of their children and in accordance with their wishes'. However, significantly, it added 'within the legal framework of the national curriculum' (DES, 1987).

Then, during the passage of the Bill in the House of Commons, Norman Tebbitt argued that:

> This Bill extends choice and responsibility. Some will choose badly or irresponsibly, but that cannot and must not be used as an excuse to deny choice and responsibility to the great majority. Today, only the wealthy have choice in education and that must be changed. Norman Tebbitt (quoted in *The Daily Telegraph*, 2 December 1987).

Yet the exercise of choice and responsibility was to be denied to the majority of parents in the field of the curriculum, where (given the exclusion of independent schools from the legislative imposition of a national curriculum and system of testing), only the wealthy would continue to have choice.

Tensions within the Education Reform Act

As a result of this, many commentators suggested that there was something of a paradox or contradiction within an Act which increasingly gave market forces their head within whole areas of policy which had previously been subject to detailed regulation and planning by central and local government, yet suddenly introduced prescription into the one area of education where hitherto there had been autonomy, save in the case of RE which was mandatory under the 1944 Education Act. Of course, that autonomy has essentially been professional autonomy rather than the autonomy of consumer choice, but why should consumer choice replace LEA and teacher judgement in most matters, but ministerial prescription take over from it in the area of curriculum decision-making. Given the tendency of most ministerial statements on the curriculum to portray the curriculum as a commodity, which presumably could be marketed just like other goods, the paradox seemed especially puzzling.

Some critics have resolved the paradox by suggesting that the devolution proposals are themselves as much about increasing central government control, at the expense of the teaching profession and local government, as they are about increasing the power of local communities which are linked with parents in the government's rhetoric (Demaine, 1988). Indeed, with the demise of any significant LEA function in relation to grant maintained schools, it can surely be argued that the role of the local people (except current parents) in relation to such schools is diminished rather than enhanced. Thus, the argument goes, the rhetoric of decentralization is a cover for centralization. The atomization of decision-making and the removal or marginalization of intervening arenas of political mobilization, such as LEAs and trade unions, effectively removes any chance of a collective challenge to the government, thus enhancing its ascendant position. And this is then consistent with an enhanced central government role in the curriculum. But again the question remains—if that is the aim, why not employ a consistent strategy? Either go for direct government management of the whole enterprise or let market forces decide the fate of everything including the curriculum.

Of course, while this paper is largely about the position of the New Right, it is also the case that, in government, the rhetoric of the New Right is tempered by other considerations (Demaine, 1988)—indeed other political forces have to be taken into account even by a Thatcher government and I will return to this point later. But yet another way of resolving the paradox has been to see different fractions within the so-called New Right itself as influencing different areas of policy. It has now become a commonplace to identify two main strands within New Right thinking—namely neo-liberal and neo-conservative. Thus, Andrew Gamble, amongst others, argues that what is distinctive about Thatcherism as a force within British conservatism is its capacity to link the neo-conservative emphasis on tradition, authority and national identity/security with an espousal of neo-liberal free market economics and the extension of its principles into whole new areas of social activity including the provision of welfare (Gamble, 1983b. See also Levitas, 1986). In analysing education, Demaine's discussion of the New Right (Demaine, 1988) focuses mainly on its neo-liberal elements, while another recent paper that recognizes this distinction places most of its emphasis on neo-conservative influences (Quicke, 1988).

As New Right ideology is based on a blend of moral and economic academic and philosophical doctrines, they are sometimes complementary, but sometimes in tension, particularly in its mediated political versions (see Edwards *et al.*, 1984, Whitty and Menter, 1989). It has also been pointed out that, provided the discourse of the New Right as political rhetoric strikes a chord and can command assent, its internal inconsistencies and its eclectic philosophical roots are something of an irrelevance (Ball forthcoming). So greater consumer power over choice and management of schools, a neo-liberal response to criticisms of LEA bureaucracies, and a national curriculum, a neo-conservative response to changes that trendy teachers are subverting traditional moral values and selling the nation short, may both resonate with popular experience and be electorally attractive even if the whole package does not add up. However, even if all this is true, there may also be a principled sense in which the various policies are at least broadly reconcilable. Gamble has suggested that the paradox of at one and the same time building a strong state through increased expenditure on the military and the apparatuses of law and order, while at the same time using state power to roll back state intervention from whole areas of social activity, does have a degree of consistency. This is because the state needs to protect the market from vested interests and restrictive practices and prevent the conditions in which it can flourish being subverted either from without or within (Gamble, 1983a). On this basis, the government's curriculum policies may not necessarily be as much at variance with its policies on the structure of the education system as is sometimes suggested, even at the level of principle. The contrast between apparent centralization in one sphere and apparent decentralization in the other may not be the paradox it at first appears. Schools which are responsive to choices made by parents in the market are believed by the government to be more likely than those administered by state bureaucrats to produce high levels of scholastic achievement, to the benefit of both individuals and the nation. The strength of the state therefore has to be used to remove anything that interferes with this process or with the development of an appropriate sense of self and nation on the part of citizens who will be making their choice in the market. Thus, not only does the traditional partnership with LEAs and teachers' unions need to be abandoned in favour of the discipline of the market, it also becomes imperative (at least in the short term) to police the curriculum to ensure that the pervasive collectivist and universalistic welfare ideology of the post-war era is restrained. In this way, support for the market, self-help, enterprise and the concept of the 'responsible' family and a common 'national identity' can be constructed. Hence, for example, whether or not Bob Dunn's intriguing suggestion that there should be compulsory teaching of free market economics was offered tongue in cheek, it may merely be an extreme example of a more general approach to the problem confronting the political project of Thatcherism within education (Hall, 1988). In other words, the overt ideology of the curriculum needs to be addressed directly before the ideology of the new structure is sufficiently developed to do its work. So, in this sense, there may actually be an ideological congruity rather than incongruity between the national curriculum proposals and other aspects of the Education Reform Act.

Neo-Liberal and Neo-Conservative Approaches to the Curriculum

Although certainly in some respects rather too neat both theoretically and empirically, this reading does actually gain credence from a study of the internal debate going on between the various pressure groups associated with the New Right. The contribution of the Hillgate Group (1986, 1987), comprising Caroline Cox, Jessica Douglas-Home, John Marks, Laurie Norcross and Roger Scruton, is particularly significant here and the apparent contradictions within it more explicable than some commentators imply (Demaine, 1988, Ball forthcoming). Rather than being the product purely of muddled thinking, these contradictions derive from an attempt to consider both short-term and long-term strategies and this is what leads to their adoption of both neo-liberal and neo-conservative policies to achieve long-term ends that will be broadly acceptable to both. Heavily influenced by neo-conservative critiques of progressivism, members of the Hillgate Group are attracted by the idea of prescription at the level of the curriculum in order to defend traditional standards and values. However, they also see parents as a potent force against progressivism and embrace—and indeed wish to extend—the government's espousal of market force in open enrolment, opting out, and so on, as the best way of improving educational standards. But their political allies in the latter cause, including some of those closest to them, such as Keith Joseph, Stuart Sexton and Dennis O'Keeffe, have argued that if market forces are to be efficacious in these other areas, why not in determining the curriculum?

O'Keeffe, for example, in what he claims to be a libertarian view of government policy (O'Keeffe, 1988), says that open enrolment, opting out and financial delegation are all entirely to the good and so is testing, in principle, providing it is conducted independently on behalf of the taxpayers and not controlled by the educational establishment. But a prescribed curriculum is both 'alien to the British tradition' (and hence presumably should be questioned by neo-conservatives as well as neo-liberals) and looks like being controlled via that 'network of in-house trading and special interest' which has controlled our quasi-syndicalized educational culture of recent years—and incidentally by the very same personnel who are especially culpable for pulling a fast one over the government with the GCSE. This group is usually referred to disparagingly by the New Right as the 'liberal educational establishment', though they sometimes suggest that its members are 'socialist' (e.g. O'Keeffe and Stoll, 1988). They fear that it could still subvert the new proposals from within and O'Keeffe would presumably see the mathematics, science and English working group reports (DES, 1988a, 1988b, 1988c), as well as the reports of the Task Group on Assessment and Testing (TGAT 1987, 1988), as vindicating this view.

Far better than anything prescribed by such groups, or even by ministers and civil servants, would be a 'free enterprise curriculum'—or that mixture of contents and styles that a 'free citizenry' plumps for. As O'Keeffe puts it himself, 'if you do not like the groceries at one supermarket, try another. The system which has utterly outperformed all others in history in the

production of a wide range of goods and services needs trying out in the field
of education too' (O'Keeffe, 1988:19). (Incidentally, I would argue that the
emphasis of the neo-liberals, like some sections of the New Left, on devising
new ways of arriving at a curriculum model rather providing an alternative
blueprint, is one of the reasons why, when it comes to concrete thinking
about the curriculum, such as that demanded of the national curriculum
working groups, the educational establishment usually gets its way).

Stuart Sexton, a former adviser to Keith Joseph and new Education
Director of the Institute of Economic Affairs, places a particularly strong
emphasis on finding an appropriate neo-liberal mechanism for determining
the curriculum. Thus, he has argued a similar case to O'Keeffe's against a
centralized and bureaucratically set 'nationalized curriculum', at the same
time as regarding the main elements of the national curriculum proposals as
what most reasonable parents would actually want. But he points out that
'for the independent schools . . . the "market" of parental demand dictates
that they do provide such a "national curriculum"'. So if a more self-
managing state sector emerges from the government's other proposals, it too
will 'have to respond to parental demand to provide an acceptable
curriculum' (Sexton, 1988a). This would allow for choice and diversity and
local variation and remove the dangers of a Secretary of State imposing a
straitjacket on enterprising schools on the say-so of the 15 or so 'experts' on
the National Curriculum Council (Sexton, 1988b). That is why Lord
Joseph moved an amendment to make the whole national curriculum
discretionary rather than mandatory, and why when that failed there were
attempts by Sexton and his colleagues to persuade the government to make
only the list of subjects mandatory and the programmes of study
discretionary. One of the arguments Joseph used in the Lords debate against
a legislated and inflexible national curriculum was that it might not meet the
needs of either non-academic or gifted children (Blackburne, 1988). And
Sexton has recently expressed concern that schools should remain free to
teach Scottish examinations or the International Baccalaureate—or even a
revived GCE 'O' level to able pupils if they wanted to and if boards wished
to offer it—and he particularly deplores those parts of the Education Reform
Act that will allow the Secretary of State, or effectively the School
Examinations and Assessment Council, to determine what examination
courses children in maintained schools can follow. He regards it as absurd
that, while independent schools may teach non-GCSE courses if they and
the parents want them to, state schools could be legally debarred from doing
so whatever the parents might wish (Sexton, 1988b, 1988c).

Sexton (1988c) calls for 'more intellectually rigorous examinations' and
his own preference for a return to GCE 'O' level is also something which the
Hillgate Group and its close associates desire (Hillgate Group, 1987; North,
1987). However, because they are strongly linked to neo-conservative forces
at the same time as having connections with advocates of a free market, they

have rather more time than Sexton or O'Keeffe for the idea of government prescribing a national curriculum in some way rather than leaving it to market forces. The Hillgate Group sympathize with the government's proposals to control the curriculum, because the eternal vigilance of parents is neither to be expected nor desired, though in the long run would prefer a proper system of examinations as a more appropriate and less contentious means of control than some of the detail of the present proposals. They firmly back the government's desire to set attainment targets, though they are less convinced about its way of developing the detailed programmes of study. But given what has happened with GCSE they are particularly supportive of the government specifying proper subjects as the basis of the curriculum and not those which are either intellectually vacuous or a cover for political indoctrination or both. One of their central concerns in this field is, at the same time as giving members of minority groups opportunities to run their own schools, to integrate them fully into the national culture and ensure a common political loyalty—in other words to provide a common framework of knowledge and values within which atomized decision making can take place. There is therefore, for example, a need for attaining targets in history that 'ensure a solid foundation in British and European history and . . . no concessions to the philosophy of the global curriculum currently advocated by the multi-culturalists' (Hillgate Group, 1987). So, although any actual programmes of study emerging from government will no doubt reflect other mediating influences, the neo-conservative strand of the New Right does clearly wish government curriculum policy to support a particular view of society and citizen. As Anne Sofer, until recently the education spokesperson of the Social and Liberal Democrats has put it, the 'draconian control' now to be exercised over the curriculum by the Secretary of State as a result of the Education Reform Act has to be seen in a context where:

> The prevailing philosophy is one that does get excited about Christianity being absolutely predominant in RE, about the need to make sure British history prevails over other sorts of history and to stamp on anything that has the label anti-racism attached to it (quoted in *Education*, 8 July 1988).

In the light of this comment, it is interesting to note that, in launching the National Curriculum Working Group on History, Kenneth Baker stated that 'the programmes of study should have at the core the history of Britain, the record of its past and, in particular, its political, constitutional and cultural heritage' (quoted in *The Times*, 14 January 1989).

The other major concern of the Hillgate Group, and associated groups such as the Campaign for Real Education, is to rid the system of the influence of the educational establishment which, of course, has traditionally regarded the curriculum as its own territory. They therefore want advisory bodies to include several members from outside the educational establishment (which they see as including DES officials and especially

HMI). While they accept O'Keeffe's argument that curriculum prescription is alien to the British educational tradition, they believe that a national curriculum is necessary so that the government, on behalf of consumers, can rid us of the influence of the educational establishment 'which prey to ideology and self-interest, is no longer in touch with the public'. It is 'time to set aside . . . the professional educators and the majority of organized teacher unions (who rather than classroom teachers) are primarily responsible for the present state of Britain's schools (Hillgate Group, 1987). Hence their broad support for a national curriculum—though not necessarily the current working groups which apparently contain 'the student radicals of the 1960s, who have marched through to leading positions in departments of education' (CRE, 1989)—at the same time as accepting with enthusiasm, though wanting to take further, all the other elements of government policy designed to devolve power to consumers. A prescribed curriculum can be used in the short term to re-educate consumers to use their new-found power responsibly and free them from dependency upon professional experts, while in the longer term the ideological changes in exercising their new responsibilities will ultimately produce changes in consciousness that will begin to render even the prescription of a national curriculum unnecessary.

So, particularly given that governments can change in our system once a curriculum appropriate for maintaining a sense of self and nation fitted for a free market society has been established, and once the last vestiges of the influence of the liberal educational establishment have been removed, the Hillgate Group might well then be content to let market forces determine the curriculum in the manner suggested by Sexton and O'Keeffe. And a similar view may actually be reflected in government policy, which implies that independent schools do not *need* legislated national curriculum because they already respond to market forces and, in most cases, teach that curriculum. The argument that they are excluded purely because they are not in receipt of public funds is less than convincing, partly because equally stringent requirements have been imposed on certain privatized utilities, but more particularly because those independent schools in the Assisted Places Scheme are effectively in receipt of public funds (in some cases now to a considerable degree) and because of this the 1980 Education Act required them to publish examination results in the same way as maintained schools. Furthermore, city technology colleges, which will certainly be in receipt of public funds, only need to adhere to the broad substance of the national curriculum presumably because, at least originally, they were conceived of as entirely new schools with new traditions set up in ways that would make them peculiarly responsive to market forces from their industrial sponsors as well as their parental clients. Grant maintained schools, though, will have to conform to the letter of the national curriculum, but then they will still be staffed by teachers schooled in and reflecting the traditions of the old LEA establishment and may need time to purge themselves of former working practices. But, in the longer term, they might be freed from such requirements as the market is trusted to undertake more of the task. In that situation, it could eventually be only LEA maintained schools that will have a highly prescriptive national curriculum.

The irony is that, if it is anything like the present national curriculum, Lord Joseph (amongst others) might well regard it as unsuitable for the particular clientele who are likely, by that stage, to be left in many LEA maintained schools (Bristol Polytechnic Education Study Group, 1989). This issue brings to light a further tension within government curriculum policy which I have discussed at greater length elsewhere (Bowe and Whitty, 1989). One of the other mediating influences on government education policy that I mentioned earlier is that of the industrial lobby. Although there is a lack of coherence both in the nature of such a group and what it does or does not require of the school curriculum, there is certainly an unresolved debate in and around government about the extent to which the national curriculum is based upon an appropriate curriculum model for the late twentieth century. In particular, there are those who ask whether it is an appropriate model for all pupils. Even with the amendment allowing certain pupils with special educational needs to be exempted from its provisions, there are many like Lord Joseph who doubt it.

The Curriculum and the Needs of Industry

Furthermore, the attack by the Hillgate Group on relevance in the curriculum appears to go against all the arguments of the last few years about the need for relevance to the needs of industry at all levels of the system and against the argument that the traditional curriculum was partly, or even largely, to blame for the decline of Britain's industrial spirit (Callaghan, 1976, Wiener, 1981, Barnett, 1986). There are many who fear that the national curriculum provisions of the Education Reform Act and the Hillgate Group's attack on relevance will spell the end of the positive innovations brought about by Technical and Vocational Education Initiative, ironically an essentially corporatist policy introduced under Keith Joseph. Jamieson and Watts have argued that, in curricular terms, the traditionally oriented Hillgate Group rather than Lord Young and the advocates of the enterprise culture have been winning the battle for the high policy ground (Jamieson and Watts, 1987). Although the initial national curriculum working group reports seemed to allay some of those fears both in content terms, but more particularly in the freedom they offered for different modes of curriculum delivery, the New Right's suspicion that they, like GCSE and TVEI, had been hi-jacked by the liberal educational establishment may perhaps be part of the explanation for Kenneth Baker's reservations about them and the amendments made to them by the National Curriculum Council and the Secretary of State (DES, 1989a, 1989b).

The continuing tensions were also evident in a recent speech by Anne Jones, director of education programmes for the Training Agency, the successor to the Manpower Services Commission/Training Commission. She emphasized that, while the national curriculum was a set of important knowledge, the process of learning offered by TVEI was also important, so that Knowledge + Process equalled Capability. But she was apparently less than convinced by the government's own commitment to the view that TVEI remains a fruitful source of ideas about the delivery of the national curriculum. Perhaps indicating some sympathy with others at the same conference who suggested that what has ultimately emerged from the NCC and Kenneth Baker from the consultation exercises over the maths and science reports looks suspiciously like the same boring old school subjects, she told her audience of TVEI teachers and co-ordinators to 'hang on in there and see what can be done. . . . The dinosaur system of schools will not do any more' (quoted in *Education*, 16 December 1988). Change would come from employers, if not from the government, she asserted.

While Roger Dale (1983) has pointed out that the industrial trainers have always had an uneasy relationship with the core groups constituting Thatcherism—and many industrialists' lack of enthusiasm for city technology colleges perhaps supports this view (Nash and Hugill, 1988)—the New Right is clearly aware that there might be a degree of embarrassment if their views were to be wholly rejected by those who claimed to speak for the nation's wealth creators. Despite the fact that the CBI was one of the few groups to welcome the original consultation document on the national curriculum virtually without reservation, CBI representatives have recently criticized some aspects of the implementation of the national curriculum, particularly the Secretary of State's revisions to the curriculum working group reports (Slee, 1989). They are particularly concerned that he has given 'too much importance to narrow academic knowledge and too little to the fostering of transferable skills and learning ability' (Jackson, 1989).

However, those associated with the Hillgate Group attempt to bridge any gap between their position and that of the government's industrial supporters by suggesting that, within the school curriculum, an emphasis on practical skills and training for life has actually become a veil for the promulgation of a 'progressive egalitarian ideology', which is ultimately a threat to enterprise (North, 1987). And echoing some of the arguments put in the Black Papers before them, they argue that the national curriculum, with its emphasis on traditional subjects, actually provides a much better grounding in the basic skills of reading, writing and comprehension which, although not taught with industrial relevance in mind, will ultimately provide industry with the properly educated recruits it currently claims to lack. Not all contributors to the Black Papers would regard a subject-based curriculum as appropriate for all pupils, though, and it is interesting in the light of our earlier discussion that Bantock, a neo-conservative in many other respects, sees differentiation between types of curricula as best arising from parental choice (Bantock, 1977).

Nevertheless, the construction of a meeting of minds between the Hillgate Group and the industrial lobby is clearly necessary if the government is to reconcile the demands of what Dale (1983) terms the industrial trainers with his old Tories, privatizers, moral entrepreneurs and populists. Indeed, any substantial failure to do so would expose one of the central assumptions in the government's approach to curriculum policy, which is that it is only professional educators in the liberal educational establishment who are out of step and that its own proposals are a distillation of what would be demanded of schools by all reasonable clients. The question of who those clients are is neatly sidestepped and the assumption made that parents and the business community have common interests (both separately and collectively) and that the combination of government prescription, parental choice and the enhanced role of parent and business governors will sort everything out.

The Consequences of a Market-Led Curriculum

This brings us to the intriguing question of what sort of curriculum a free market approach as advocated by O'Keeffe and Sexton would actually produce. Would parents opt for something akin to the national curriculum? Would it be regarded favourably by industry? And, would it be regarded favourably by the pupils, whose absence from most contemporary discussions of consumer choice (with the exception of the Hillgate Group as it happens) is interesting in itself? At the moment, we cannot answer those questions because we do not have a free market situation in the curriculum and the government is not actually proposing one. We can only rely on data from what parents tell us they want from a school and what we know about how far that actually influences choice. A future task is to analyse the mass of data on these issues which we collected from both private and public sectors in the course of our recent research on the Assisted Places Scheme (Edwards *et al.*, 1989). Then we might have some clearer answers as to what sort of curriculum a free market might produce. In the meantime, what follows is based on a very preliminary analysis of that data to help point up some of these issues which seem to be raised by the idea of letting the market set the curriculum.

Certainly amongst the parents of pupils likely to be interested in assisted places, there was widespread demand for a traditional curriculum model. And amongst many of those parents, a suspicion of too overt a vocational or even pre-vocational orientation to education. This was certainly the view of the heads of many comprehensive schools and, of course, it would be primarily in the light of their conception of what the market wanted that schools would construct their curricula in a free market situation. We even came across heads who had avoided TVEI because they saw it, rightly or wrongly, as watering down the curriculum that had most appeal to parents. And schools which saw themselves as wanting to compete with independent schools for academically able pupils were very much influenced by their model and some of them admitted that this might well be to the disadvantage of other market segments that they, unlike the independent schools, were expected to serve. It does seem likely, then, that the cultural pull of the public or grammar school curriculum (or rather the public perception of that curriculum) would distort the market with consequences that would not please the advocates of relevance as an organizing principle for the curriculum. (In this context, it will be interesting to see how the curricula of city technology colleges develop).

The head of what we have called in our study Thomas Darby High School, an inner city TVEI school with very few pupils with VRQ scores over 105 and badly affected by falling rolls, told us recently:

> What I think we have got is parents who are opting for an education system which they experienced 20 or 30 years ago. When Kenneth Baker talks about needing to recruit more people for science and technology and when we get vast amounts of money spent on records of achievement, TVEI and so on, it isn't the schools who are dragging their feet on this, it is the parent expectations that are dragging on this. I mean . . . the parents who send their children to the other schools predominantly want something that is very safe, secure, dull and predictable to make them happy—and a school (like this) that is offering them something else is seen to be experimental and threatening (Fieldwork interview, October 1988).

On the other hand, this head felt that his own school's parents were more enthusiastic about TVEI than they were about most things, but then they were largely inner city parents who had chosen the school because it was local rather than on any specific curricular considerations. In other words, most of those who had made positive curriculum choices had gone elsewhere.

That sort of dynamic was certainly clear in one of our three local study areas and it was present to some extent, though in a less clearcut way, in the other two. If it proved to be at all typical, then O'Keeffe's free enterprise curriculum might produce a situation in which inner city schools were the only ones experimenting in curricular terms. Now Lord Joseph would presumably argue that that was a good thing, because the market would then create a relevant curriculum for those unable to cope with the traditional academic one. On this model, schools with an unattractive curriculum for any market segment would eventually wither away. This assumes that curriculum provision is an important factor in choice of schools, whereas in fact many schools are currently chosen because they are local or because friends are going to them. This is particularly true in the case of those parents whose children attended schools like Thomas Darby and, in such cases, the discipline of the market might not have any clearly beneficial effects in curricular terms and it would certainly not necessarily limit the freedom of teachers to experiment. This may well explain the government's current rejection of the free enterprise approach to the curriculum for such schools.

Indeed, we saw earlier that, in the absence of a totally market centred approach to curriculum policy and given the mixed mode approach currently favoured by government, it might well be that in practice, in the longer term, LEA schools like those in the inner city could actually become the only ones to have the national curriculum imposed on them, while others arrived at it through market forces. We need then to consider how far such an imposition would be desirable. The Hillgate Group would presumably justify it on the basis that some inner city dwellers are amongst those most in need of a prescribed initiation into a common national culture and a common political loyalty, because they 'might not yet be aware of its strengths and advantages' (Hillgate Group, 1987:4). But, whatever one thinks about that particular argument, even opponents of a national curriculum on the left would need to think carefully about the position of pupils left in under-resourced inner city schools if there was no national curriculum. If everyone else was getting the national curriculum through parental choice, then the arguments in terms of equity might well point in the direction of insisting that those pupils had access to it as well, rather than providing them with a separate curriculum base on relevance, particularly if parents had not expressed a positive preference for it—and perhaps even if they had. Otherwise, Martyn Shipman's strictures of ten years ago about trendy teachers experimenting on other people's children while exposing their own to the most traditional curriculum imaginable might well remain appropriate (Shipman, 1980). Even so, this raises a major dilemma, since treating people who are different in the same way can actually be a major source of inequality itself, and this certainly needs to be taken very seriously when addressing the modes of delivery of any national curriculum.

The issue of what is appropriate curriculum provision in residential or 'sink' schools becomes a particularly significant one in the context of current government policies because the non-curricular elements of the Education Reform Act are eventually likely to produce an even more hierarchical and differentiated system of schooling than we have at the moment, with independent schools at the top, with city technology colleges and grant maintained schools and perhaps voluntary aided schools below them, with county maintained schools at the bottom (Bristol Polytechnic Education Study Group, 1989). In that situation, LEA or 'council' schools would again become the paupers of the system and the preserve of those unable or unwilling to compete in the market. As such, they might well become straightforward institutions of social control for the inner cities, though the legitimacy of the system and the notion of an open society would still be maintained by devices such as the Assisted Places Scheme, which can be seen as legitimating inequality by ostensibly offering opportunities to 'worthy' disadvantaged children to 'escape' from their backgrounds, while actually (on the evidence available so far) attracting mainly middle class children and enhancing the market appeal of the private sector (Edwards *et al.*, 1989).

The head of another inner city school we interviewed in connection with the Assisted Places research reported that a leading member of the neo-liberal tendency of the New Right had said openly at a meeting of heads recently that any market produces casualties and that the children left in 'sink' schools in the period before they went to the wall would unfortunately be amongst them (Fieldwork interview at Knotley High School, October 1988). Some people, as Norman Tebbitt said in the quotation cited earlier, make 'irresponsible' choices and, in this case, children will presumably have to suffer for their parents' irresponsibility. Any suggestion that their choices might be structured by influences beyond the family, for which compensation should be made, has been largely rejected by the government because, as Kenneth Baker said in a speech at Crawley during the passage of the Education Reform Act, 'for too long we have accepted socio-economic causes for why families should not be doing certain things' (quoted in *The Financial Times*, 12 December 1987). Hence the government's guidelines for funding formulae for local management of schools place little stress on socio-economic factors of the sort that have influenced education funding formulae in many urban LEAs in the past (Bristol Polytechnic Education Study Group, 1989).

As market forces come to define all aspects of provision other than the curriculum, those in inner city schools may become increasingly disadvantaged. As a leading Conservative critic of the government's market-oriented initiatives pointed out when they were first mooted, they 'all help most those children with parents best able to play the system to escape from poor schools. They do nothing for the quality of education of (those) who remain behind' (Argyropulo, 1986). This explained his broad support, and that of the Conservtive Education Association, for a national curriculum to offset the worst effects of the other government policies on these schools. Yet the government's own insistence that such schools should teach the national curriculum could also be seen as a cynical ploy to make it appear that there was a measure of equal treatment for all pupils when the structures that emanate from the other measures all conspired to deny it having any meaningful effect.

However, that does not seem a good reason for saying that it would be better to strip away the legitimating veil of the national curriculum and let the market do its best—or worst. One of the results of market oriented social and economic policies is, as the Archbishop of Canterbury's Commission on the inner city pointed out, that a distinct group separated from the rest of society emerges (Archbishop of Canterbury's Commission, 1985). It thereby becomes further divided even from the rest of the working class and its political movements which in the past have fought, amongst other things, for a common system of education. In the current, virtually universalistic, system of state provision, it is at least possible to conceive of groups opposed to the injustices of the system combining to fight for gains that individually they could never hope to win. The atomization of decision-making that is a feature of current government policies on open enrolment and so on threatens not only negative conception of collectivism associated with inhuman state bureaucracies; it also constitutes an attack on the very notion that collective action is a legitimate way of struggling for social justice.

In that situation, one can argue that, however cynical its imposition might appear, we should be thankful that the national curriculum is there as the one remaining symbol of a common education system and specifiable entitlement which people can struggle collectively to improve, rather than letting all provision emerge from the individual exercise of choice (or non-choice) in the market-place. To that extent, the influence of the neo-conservatives within the New Right may ultimately prove fortuitous. But, of course, for those who reject both the neo-liberal and the neo-conservative visions of the world, the present national curriculum will need changing. Even then, it will not be enough to work together to develop an alternative version of the national curriculum, and certainly not enough to substitute Keynes or Marx in Bob Dunn's statement which heads this paper. The much more daunting task will undoubtedly be to find ways of developing an alternative structure for the education system which is consistent with an alternative political project and which will command electoral consent. What does seem quite clear is that neither welfare state versions of collectivism nor the atomized market approach of Thatcherism will serve that purpose and that a national curriculum delivered in either of those contexts will effectively be discredited however good it appears on paper. And, to that extent, it is the neo-liberals who are right to remind us of the importance of considering what are the appropriate democratic mechanisms for arriving at a national curriculum, rather than just what we as 'experts' from the liberal education establishment think it ought to consist of.

Note

1. This paper was first presented at the International Sociology of Education conference at Newman College Birmingham 3–5 January 1989. Parts of the paper draw upon work carried out with Tony Edwards and John Fitz, in the context of our study of the Assisted Places Scheme (ESRC Award No. C00230036), and with Ian Menter, Nick Clough, Veronica Lee and Tony Trodd, my fellow members of the Bristol Polytechnic Education Study Group. However, none of these colleagues should be held responsible for the arguments put forward in this paper.

References

Archbishop of Canberbury's Commission on Urban Priority Areas (1985) *Faith in the City* (London: Church House Publishing).

Argyropulo, D. (1986) Inner city quality, *The Times Educational Supplement*, 1 August.

Ball, S. (forthcoming) *Politics and Policy-making in Education* (London: Routledge).

Bantock, G. (1977) An alternative curriculum, in C. B. Cox and R. Boyson (eds) *Black Paper 1977* (London: Temple Smith), pp. 78–86.

Barnett, C. (1986) *The Audit of War* (London: Macmillan).

Blackburne, L. (1988) Joseph's curriculum revolt fails, *The Times Educational Supplement*, 6 May.

Bowe, R. and Whitty, G. (1989) The re-opening of the GCSE 'Settlement': Recent developments in the politics of school examinations'. *British Journal of Sociology of Education*, 10(4).

Bristol Polytechnic Education Study Group (1989) Restructuring the education system?, in L. Bash and D. Colby (eds) *The Education Reform Act* (London: Cassell).

Callaghan, J. (1976) Towards a national debate, *Education* 148 (17).

Campaign for Real Education (1989) Cause for concern? *Newsletter* 3 (1).

Dale, R. (1983) Thatcherism and Education, in J. Ahier and M. Flude (eds), *Contemporary Education Policy* (London: Croom Helm), pp. 233–255.

Demaine, J. (1988) Teachers' work, curriculum and the New Right, *British Journal of Sociology of Education*, 9 (3), pp. 247–264.

DES (Department of Education and Science) (1987) *Grant Maintained Schools: Consultation Paper* (London: Department of Education and Science)

DES (1988a) *Mathematics for Ages 5 to 16* (London: Department of Education and Science).

DES (1988b) *Science for Ages 5 to 16* (London: Department of Education and Science).

DES (1988c) *English for Ages 5 to 11* (London: Department of Education and Science).

DES (1989a) *Mathematics in the National Curriculum* (London: HMSO).

DES (1989b) *Science in the National Curriculum* (London: HMSO).

Edwards, A., Fulbrook, M. and Whitty, G. (1984) The tate and the independent sector: Policies, ideologies and theories, in L. Barton and S. Walker (eds) *Social Crisis and Educational Research* (London: Croom Helm) pp. 118–150.

Edwards, A., Fitz, J. and Whitty, G. (1989) *The State and Private Education: A Study of the Assisted Places Scheme* (Lewes: Falmer Press).

Gamble, A. (1983a) *Education under Monetarism* (London: World University Service).

Gamble, A. (1983b) Thatcherism and Conservative politics, in S. Hall and M. Jacques (eds), *The Politics of Thatcherism* (London: Lawrence and Wishart) pp. 109–131.

Hall, S. (1988) *The Hard Road to Renewal: Thatcherism and the Crisis of the Left* (London: Verso).

Hillgate Group (1986) *Whose Schools? A Radical Manifesto* (London: Hillgate Group).

Hillgate Group (1987) *The Reform of British Education* (London: Claridge Press)

Jackson, M. (1989) CBI struggles to 'save' curriculum from Baker. *The Times Educational Supplement*, 24 March.

Jamieson, I. and Watts, T. (1987) Squeezing out enterprise. *The Times Educational Supplement*, 18 December.

Levitas, R. (ed.) (1986) *The Ideology of the New Right* (Oxford: Polity Press).

Nash, I and Hugill, B. (1988) Industrial giant spurns Baker CTC approach, *The Times Educational Supplement*, 27 May.

North, J. (ed.) (1987) *The GCSE: An Examination* (London: Claridge Press).

O'Keeffe, D. (1988) A critical look at a national curriculum and testing: a libertarian view, paper presented to American Educational Research Association, New Orleans, April.

O'Keeffe, D. and Stoll, P. (1988) 'Postscript' to S. Sexton (ed.) *GCSE: A Critical Analysis* (Croydon: IEA Education Unit).

Quicke, J. (1988) The 'New Right' and education, *British Journal of Educational Studies*, 26 (1), pp. 5–20.

Sexton, S. (1988a) No Nationalization Curriculum, *The Times*, 8 May.

Sexton, S. (1988b) Squeezing out choice at the grassroots, *Education*, 9 September.

Sexton S. (ed.) (1988c) *GCSE: A Critical Analysis* (Croydon: IEA Education Unit).

Shipman, M. (1980) The limits of positive discrimination, in M. Marland (ed.) *Education for the Inner City* (London: Heinemann), pp. 69–92.

Slee, P. (1989) Redundant reforms, *Education*, 13 January.

TGAT (Task Group on Assessment and Testing) (1987) *A Report* (London: Department of Education and Science).

TGAT (1988) *Three Supplementary Reports* (London: Department of Education and Science).

Whitty, G. and Menter, I. (1989) Lessons of Thatcherism: Education policy in England and Wales, 1979–88, *Journal of Law and Society*, **16** (1), pp. 42–64.

Wiener, M. (1981) *English Culture and the Decline of the Industrial Spirit 1850–1980* (Cambridge: Cambridge University Press).

10

Explaining Economic Decline and Teaching Children About Industry: some unintended continuities?*

JOHN AHIER

The Education Reform Act has performed at least one important task for politically conscious educationalists and for educationally aware politicians and industrialists. It has opened up directly for discussion and investigation the whole question about what future citizens should be taught, how, and in what proportions. The education debate which began well before the Bill's passage through Parliament, and will continue during subsequent stages of implementation, could do more to raise awareness about the social and political issues surrounding educational knowledge than any number of books and seminars on the social nature or origins of the curriculum. A timid reaction may be to regret the 'politicization' of the schools. Those who thought that the curriculum was only the concern of themselves and their professional judgement may feel upset. It is true that the extent and levels of consultation have been restricted and superficial. But few could now believe that the notion of the central state deciding on what was taught in schools is foreign to the English way of doing things.

At least one of the tasks which must now be done is to re-consider some of the foundations of the present political debate about education, testing them for strength, to see whether they can hold up subsequent developments in educational thinking on the political Right, Left or Centre.

One foundation upon which some of the current advocacy of educational as well as social economic policies is built is the general thesis concerning Britain's anti-industrial culture. This explanation of national economic decline has existed in various forms during the last twenty years or more. It can be expressed in the crudest lounge bar cliches about the work-shy English, and it has formed the basis of quite sophisticated research and

*Specially commissioned for this volume. © The Open University, 1990.

commentary on national culture and education. We have no way of knowing if there are any connections between these two levels but, as Hall and others have shown, (Hall, 1987) there does seem to have been a use made of some of the hitherto academically supported notions of a national anti-industrialism by politicians of all parties over the last two decades. Naturally, once the seeds of suspicion are sown regarding the nation's culture it is not long before its institutions of cultural transmission come under attack.

What I want to do here is to criticize the cultural explanations of national economic decline and to show, by comparison with some other types of explanation, that they have a kind of affinity with discourses within state schooling. In spite of being mistaken these cultural explanations can be used to justify certain educational developments in a direct and simple way, and their rhetoric can be easily assimilated into contemporary educational debate. Other kinds of explanation create interesting dilemmas and problems for educators which I shall attempt to eludicate.

The test which may have had the most effect in developing and sustaining the cultural explanation of economic decline is Martin Wiener's *English Culture and the Decline of the Industrial Spirit, 1850–1980* (1981). Soon after it was published this book had a programme in the *World in Action* television series devoted to it, *The Betrayal of British Industry*, (November, 1982) in which both the future leader of the Labour Party and a Conservative minister voiced support for Wiener's thesis. Ralf Dahrendorf, too, used it in his series *Dahrendorf on Britain* (BBC television, January, 1985) to show both why Britain had declined and why it had not made the same political mistakes as other countries. Subsequently Wiener's thesis has been used by many political commentators and academics.

In his book Wiener (1981) documents numerous instances of anti-industrialism and anti-urbanism from a whole range of cultural practices, arguing that these sentiments and values are particularly English. From the Gothic revival onwards he sees English culture continually expressing a deep suspicion of industry and commerce. Dickens, for example, rejected the values of commercial society, as did Ruskin and Arnold. The very image of the notion—Old England—he saw as constructed after 1900 by nostalgic reference to thatched cottages and rural existence, and village life was consistently idealized. Middle class English suburban architecture provided mostly farmhouses and yeomen's cottages, and the politicians from Baldwin to Churchill played upon a popular nostalgia. Wiener considers that, by the First World War, fascination with the old country life had spread throughout the middle class and anti-industrialism had invaded all of the national culture.

In the second half of the book Wiener goes on to show the effects of this development. It has meant that a set of values has ensured that low status has been given to industrialists, who lost confidence and had to suffer, not only the attacks from the political Left, but also the condescension of both the learned professions and the City (p. 129). Those who stayed in industry lacked commitment to business and tried to live the lives of country gentlemen.

Wiener explains this apparent national cultural aberration by tracing it back to what has been called Britain's 'exceptionalism' (Ingham, 1984, p. 3). To blame was the fact that, in this country, a bourgeois, industrial elite never really triumphed. Instead an accommodation was reached between the aristocracy and bourgeoisie, with the old rentier aristocracy holding on to cultural hegemony. This meant that the very class which should have been pressed on with the entrepreneurial spirit became compromised, as did the whole nation.

In reading Wiener one cannot escape some of the great similarities between his arguments and an earlier Left critique of the national culture by Perry Anderson (Anderson, 1964, 1968). Indeed Wiener acknowledges how this form of cultural criticism knows no political boundaries by including Anderson with some Right wing commentators like Joseph and Worsthorne (p. 8). If some of the Right have thought that the original class compromise failed to make this country safe for successful capitalism, Anderson and others on the Left bemoaned the fact that it inhibited the production of a true, holistic, bourgeois world view which could only be challenged by a home-produced Marxism (Anderson, 1968).

All this may seem both confusing and possibly inconsequential were it not for the fact that over the last ten years institutional changes have been brought about, the rationale for which is to be found on the Right hand side of this interpretation of cultural history. Attempts to turn educators into market calculators, to bring enterprise culture into schools and colleges and to replace state dependence with entrepreneurial vigour are the Right's political answers to a nation seen to be in decline.

It is timely, therefore, to consider critically this social explanation of an economic fact and to ask what light it can throw on the study of education and contemporary curriculum change.

To begin with, the social and cultural history which is presupposed in the Wiener thesis and others like it is highly problematic. Over twenty years ago E. P. Thompson suggested some serious problems with Anderson's work (Thompson, 1965) but Wiener took little notice. The latter uses concepts like 'accommodation', 'adaptation', and 'absorption' (pp. 9–10) to describe the relationship between the cultures of the aristocracy and bourgeoisies, thus presuming that there were at a crucial point in the nineteenth century two quite distinct and essential sets of values and ways of life. It is interesting that this is not the first time that writers who have sought to describe the national personality have been drawn by this human metaphor to find in history two parents for their creature. In more confident times it was thought that the English character was the ideal product of the freedom-loving Anglo-Saxons and the discipline of the Normans (Fletcher and

Kipling, 1911). Such approaches require both the simplistic reduction of a group's culture to a set of values and a belief that one group's apparently predominant values were set and generated internally before contact with the other.

Problems with any notions of economic class categories as agents with their own internal cultures have been well rehearsed in theory (Coward, 1977). Problems with Wiener's particular characterization of the industrial bourgeoisie and its culture have been pointed out in a recent set of studies of the English middle class in the last century (Wolff and Seed, 1988). Here it is noted, with some surprise, that in spite of Thompson's assault on the original thesis concerning the union of aristocratic traditionalism and bourgeois empiricism these notions of class-cultural compromise continue to be held. Seed and Wolff comment, 'Indeed, in many respects they have become a new intellectual orthodoxy in some—predominantly Conservative—political circles' (p. 3).

For these historians the weakness of the whole thesis is that it relies for its characterization of industrial bourgeois culture on secondary sources. Descriptions of this culture tend to come from its critics like Pugin, Ruskin or Arnold, or from the fictions of Dickens, as much as from any real study of depth and complexity of that class itself. Indeed, when one considers the great range of backgrounds as well as political and religious beliefs of the archetypal entrepreneurs, the Lancashire cotton masters, one cannot believe that their success could ever depend upon original enterprise culture of industrial spirit (Howe, 1984; Crouzet, 1985). As Gunn argues, the evidence is that there was no industrial middle class in England which was distinct from the professions, for example, but rather a grouping with sufficient mobility between law, commerce and industry to maintain its local power bases and access to wealth (Gunn, 1988, p. 32).

If recent research is opening up the presuppositions about the middle class culture which informed Wiener's book then there has already been considerable doubt thrown on the characterization of what may be called the other side. Thompson, among others, has shown fairly conclusively that, the landed aristocracy, if it had ever been un-capitalist or anti-capitalist had certainly moved more than half way towards embracing capitalist methods and ideals by the mid-nineteenth century; hence it is misleading to argue that the drive towards landed status, and the adoption of gentlemanly values, inevitably sapped 'the industrial spirit . . .' (Thompson, 1984, p. 208).

There are not only some shortcomings in the social history upon which the Wiener thesis is based, but the model of the social and historical explanation used is very dubious, especially in the way it understands the place of educational institutions in social change. Like some of the other explanations of Britain's economic decline outlined in Coates and Hillard (1986) Wiener's approach tends to assume that an industrial society should proceed along an unswerving path of economic growth. The space for the construction of his 'anti-industrial culture' is given by the comparison of an explained notion of the *normal* stages of national economic development with the actual industrial progress of Britain. Thus functionalist concepts like 'lag' and 'residue' are used to explain why this particular national economy has moved at a different pace from others. Unfortunately, all the approaches to the British economy which depend on notions of its 'exceptionalism' make it difficult to grasp the specific effects of the City, for example, what it does for international capitalism, and how it relates to both the state and industry (viz., Ingham, 1984).

Wiener's actual social analysis is concerned with identifying an all-powerful social elite, born of the rentier aristocracy and the industrial bourgeoisie, which was completely homogeneous in terms of culture, values and education by the end of Queen Victoria's reign. In his book, however, this elite is vaguely defined, at one time tautologically becoming all those who espoused the values of the elite (p. 159), at another time being defined by sources of income, by wealth, occupation and education (p. 158). Other studies of the elites have usually been concerned with the empirical investigation of the degrees to which various groupings are interconnected, the extent of elite coherence and so on (Stanworth and Giddens, 1974), but Wiener deals in holisms, more associated, perhaps, with forms of Hegelian Marxism. His elite has a 'world view', (the title of Part II of his book), with all the presuppositions of unity. It is this world view which became the unchallenged cultural essence of the nation via what might be called a 'seepage' theory of elite influence. His approach is perfectly expressed in the following quote:

> Elites have disproportionate influence upon both the effective climate of opinion and the conduct of affairs. The values of the directing strata, particularly in a stable, cohesive society like modern Britain, tend to permeate society as a whole and to take on the colour of national values, and of a general mentalité (p. 5).

The role of educational institutions in such an implicit society theory is clear. They both consolidate the elite and diffuse its values throughout society. Wiener sees the public schools as devoted to separating the sons of the industrial middle class from their economic roots by assimilating them into the ways of the leisured, landed gentlemen via a liberal, non-scientific, anti-industrial curriculum (pp. 16–22). Subsequently the grammar and state schools came to emulate these high status institutions because they were developed, after 1902, by the products of that public school system. Recently this aspect of Wiener's work has been extended to show that the present attempts to change the educational system towards commercial awareness and a pro-industry stance is bound to fail because the system has always embodied and perpetuated 'the values of British society's dominant elites' (Mathieson and Bernbaum, 1988, p. 127). In this paper one can detect some slight differences and developments. At times Mathieson and

Bernbaum admit there has been some opposition, and they refer to a plurality of elites, although they see them all characterized by anti-industrialism. Through a consideration of Coleridge they show up the links between that anti-industrialism and the Christian aims of both public and state education in the nineteenth and twentieth centuries. They investigate too, how a particular form of progressive education in England reflected literary, spiritual values, with little or no commitment to science or intellect. But both these writers, and Wiener himself, do seem to grossly oversimplify the original functions of the public schools and the ways in which the content of curricula in any schools develop and influence teachers and pupils.

To begin with, they overstate the function of the major public schools as that of assimilation of the middle class into English, aristocratic, landed values. If one must seek a central function for these places then it would be more likely to be the teaching of leadership, and the preparation for the use of power. To quote Gunn (1988),

> 'if the notion of leadership is stripped of extraneous aristocratic connotations then it is possible to comprehend the Victorian public school for what it actually was; an educational system finely adjusted to meet the directive needs of a class society that was at once agricultural, industrial, commercial and above all imperial. Public school education proved itself capable of accommodating different socio-economic interests by concentrating on the major interest they held in common, the exercise of power' (Gunn, 1988 pp. 35–6).

Indeed, the public schools were no more devoted to the success of a single anti-industrial, ruralist, literary and Christian culture than the middle class educational institutions of the first half of the nineteenth century were devoted to an entrepreneurial, scientific alternative. Visible curricula, to the extent that they are divided into subject, are likely to be much more ambiguous.

What approach to the content of school curricula does the Wiener thesis suggest? His means of establishing the existence of an anti-industrial and anti-urban world view was to itemize numerous examples of the essential sentiments. If we were to substantiate his theory as far as education was concerned we would have to study the content of various school curricula to detect the presence of these sentiments, looking, for example, at how industry was portrayed, and, indeed, whether it was referred to at all. In his inimitable style this is exactly what David Marsland did in his critical analysis of introductory sociology textbooks (Marsland, 1988). Following exactly Wiener's explanation of economic decline (pp. 23–4) he vigorously pursued what he considered to be a whole set of biases in these books, and he did this by considering what it omitted, what is given insufficient emphasis or a negative evaluation, and what is unfairly described. Thus he found a constant neglect or negation of enterprise, competition, advertising, property and profit, and students got no contact with 'economic reality' (p. 50).

In some ways Marsland makes a number of telling points. In much of popular sociology there has been very little concern for such things as economic policy, the different nature of economic institutions in various states which may account, in part, for their different economic performances, and other important areas of economic understanding. It is the case where there has been a tendency to consider economic structures only from the point of view of their class-producing functions (Ahier, 1983, p. 12). But his points are not really made to correct imbalances within an academic discipline or even to encourage the economic education of students of social science, but to promote one bias against another, and to instil respect for Britain's 'established and requisite economic and political institutions' (p. 29). Marsland wants the textbooks to give 'a positive account of British society and its economic institutions which is powerfully justified by all the relevant facts' (p. 58). This is indeed an extreme version and interpretation of the Wiener thesis. Anyone with a concern about national economic performance—and Marsland himself admits there has been a 'drift towards national bankruptcy' (p. 25)—could hardly be serious in thinking that British economic performances have been the anti-enterprise values as found in sociology textbooks. It is a sign of the level of the debate represented in this book, and currently within the popular press, that Marsland can suggest that we should study 'the market' in sociology because it is the 'primary institution of the economy of liberal-capitalist societies' (p. 45). Studying 'the market' as a single institution is likely to be as unpromising as studying 'the state' as a single unified body or 'the people' as the undifferentiated beneficiary and supporter of socialism.

What is mistaken in this whole enterprise is the belief that you can track down some socially damaging cultural element, be it racism or ruralism, by the content analysis of educational or other texts, and they put it right by re-writing the books, reversing the values and including the excluded. Marsland ends his attack with the inevitable check lists, very similar, in their way, to the ones produced by those who have pursued racism and sexism by the same methods. More sinister is Marsland's reliance on an implicit state power for inspection and enforcement (p. 197).

If the belief that English culture had become generally imbued with elements of anti-industrialism over a long period was correct, and if one thought that content analysis was a satisfactory means of investigating texts, then one might well expect to find these elements in the textbooks of the nation's schools. Given that sociology is a recent and perhaps temporary visitor to the English secondary school curriculum one might look at the texts of two established subjects which could be relevant, history and geography.

When looking at history books used in elementary schools, and later in the primary schools in England from the 1900s to the 1960s such a reading of these books will certainly provide evidence for the Wiener thesis. On the other hand it will also provide hints that the thesis is at fault and that the other ideological tasks performed by schools were contradictory in appearance and ambivalent in outcome.

In these books one can find substantial support for the existence of one aspect of anti-industrialism. They abound with ruralist sentiments and generally portray urban life, especially in industrial cities, as dirty and miserable.[1] By way of contrast the Anglo-Saxon period was presented as a particularly favourable time, when original English people could farm and enjoy country pleasures. Children were so often told that it was the 'country air' which was so beneficial compared with 'town air', which, regardless of period or place, was always foul. When visual images of town and country were used the rural scenes were viewed from above, with villages, fields, cottages and domestic life spread out below. The towns, by contrast, were represented from street level, with all their inhospitable dirt and vulgar business. Thus, when it comes to explaining to the child reader the complex process of industrialization, the key indicator used was a particularly regrettable *loss*, of air, land and homeliness.

Significantly the contrasts between the rural past and what came after it were most extreme when the texts compared the lives of children in the two periods and localities. Quite ignoring the facts of rural child labour they described the idyllic life of rural children and contrasted it with that of town children in factories and streets, whose only hope was the coming of Lord Shaftesbury and the state schools in which these textbooks came to be used (Ahier, 1988, pp. 112–13). There is no support here for industrial—urban life. Indeed, in the books written and used after the Second World War it is as though the urban-industrial period of British history was over, and the key signs of modern Britain were taken to be the New Towns and suburbs of a planned landscape. New domestic scenes were depicted, safe and at ease in the housing estates of social democratic England.

Surely these images found in English history textbooks could be taken as undeniable evidence of the anti-industrial culture which they expressed and into which they initiated the child-readers? There are, however, other ways of reading these texts. First, the way industrialization is explained may be mistaken, yet it does hold up for adulation all the virtues of enterprise and inventiveness. In fact the whole process of industrialization has been explained in terms of the hard work and diligence of individual men. If squires, farmers and yeomen were the heroes of rural life, Arkwright, Stephenson, Cartwright, Hargreaves and Watt were the men who brought us strength, wealth and employment.[2] These explanations, together with their descriptions of the machines which were thought to be so important, may not have given children any adequate understanding of the economic, social and political process of industrialization. They might have given magical accounts of wealth creation as the business of individual men, yet in that respect they are quite consistent with the presuppositions of the advocates of an enterprise culture.

It could still be argued that this adulation of the enterprising inventor stands out simply because there is so much appreciation of rural figures and rural settings. There are, however, other ways of understanding the predominance of the latter besides seeing them as cumulative expressions of national anti-industrialism. There are what might be called *internal* reasons for presenting the past in the ways the books have done. For example, one cannot escape the feeling that rural, domestic life was described in the way it was because it was thought to suit the minds and inclinations of child-readers. Many of the books were organized in series to be followed chronologically, and the chronology of the nation was linked to pre-given notions of the stages of children's development. Because it has been thought for so long that children below a certain age could not, and should not, grasp the abstractions of money, markets, capital, investment and profit the development of capitalism has had to be 'belittled' for them and made concrete by the images of urbanization and invention. Mathieson and Bernbaum (1988), in their extension of the Wiener thesis, thought that educational progressivism was tainted by English anti-industrialism, but the most effective development of progressivism took the form of a child-centredness which was built on notions of the nature of childhood and its stages, and so many writers on children's development have thought that they are best nurtured in direct contact with nature. The peculiarity of these histories for children appear to have more to do with the gentility of the child-centred pedagogue than with the ruralism of a whole national culture.

More doubt still is cast upon the notion of the school curriculum expressing the national culture as characterized by Wiener if one considers the textbooks of another subject. In geography books we find an emphasis on the 'natural' ways of teaching children the subject by contact with nature. Much is made of observing the weather and walking in the countryside (Ahier, 1988, pp. 129–30). When considering what was often called 'the homeland' the greatest prominence is given to the farmer, but the books also went to great lengths to present the nation as the 'workshop of the world'. When children have been introduced to the differences between 'us' and 'them', 'here' and 'there', it is the urban and industrial which has been taken as the positive distinguishing quality of the nation. Children in the past have been told frequently that the natural gifts of a temperate climate and adequate supplies of coal have made 'us' what we are—a powerful, civilized, *industrial* country. The travels of imaginary child-characters in many of the books include visits to coal mines, steel works and cotton factories, as well as farms, all interconnected within a national homeland, a national division of labour and an exchange of equivalents.

When a world geography was presented to children, a set of contrasts played upon 'our' industrialization' and 'their' primitiveness. Again, because of certain internal educational commitments to a regional geography and its climatic determinations, and because it was thought that children would be fascinated by the odd and the different, it was other countries which were always represented by their agriculture and other people who were seen as close—too close—to nature. Certainly the idea that Britain was the only industrialized society, or that other countries were only too happy to 'help' us by sending us their produce, was a gross misunderstanding of the evolving place of the British economy during the long period when these books were in use, but one could hardly see such representations of 'us' and 'them' as springing from any essential anti-industrialism.

The problems found with the Wiener thesis and its application to school knowledge can be used to make three more general points with regard to the study of contemporary curricula and their associated texts and materials.

First, it would appear difficult, if not impossible to maintain any notion of a singular curriculum as an expression of a culture, whether of a nation or a social class. (Wiener's thesis depends on the former becoming the latter). The difficulty cannot be solved by merely adding other influences, or by seeing the curriculum as an arena of cultural conflict between groups differentiated outside of schools and education. Such an approach may throw light on contemporary struggles between those who seek a more 'practical' curriculum and an 'education for capability, and those who want to preserve the national culture via traditional standards, but it tends to ignore factors internal to pedagogy and the institutions of schooling. The chronological organization of children and the related theories of cognitive development which have been integral to the enterprise of state schooling must be seen as crucially determining what can be taught, how, in what order and to whom. Thus what might be seen as elements of a national anti-urbanism at one level may also be considered as attempts to charm the innocent and natural young child and use their innate curiosity. In a similar way, the persistence of certain images within the textbooks used in the nation's schools may have more to do with the way internal pedagogic conventions of representation appear to be sustained by educational publishing practices than by any national cultural lag or lasting aristocratic embrace. In school publishing the standard texts and original images have been in use, with minor revisions, for very extended periods of time. It is not only because this is profitable for the publishers, but also because of the way conceptions of the child-reader, in a sense, *polices* the texts which can be produced. Thus, for example, although there has been some considerable support recently for teaching primary schoolchildren about industry and work, the materials to help teachers do this have been very limited, and few have been able to present even the simplest economic concepts to a young readership.

Second, if the curriculum and curricular materials *express* no unity then we should not expect that they *address* any unity either. So often critical analysis of educational knowledge presumes that certain materials will have similar effects on all children. When different effects are admitted, then those will be accounted for purely in terms of the relevance or irrelevance of the materials and ideas to children of different classes, races or localities. For example, one of the most public criticisms of the so-called traditional curriculum in the 1970s by educationalists like Midwinter (e.g. Midwinter, 1971) was that the content was quite inappropriate for children of the inner city. It was argued that the issues dealt within, say, English or history were unrealistic, even whimsical, and too distant from the everyday lives of the children from the urban working class. Following significant developments in the analysis of the relationship between author, reader and text we can no longer accept, either that curriculum content has any necessary direct effect upon pupils conceived as passive recipients in the ways previously presumed, or that the closer the content is to the everyday life of the child-subject then the more effective it will be. Research on the way comics and school stories work for girls (Walkerdine, 1984; Frith, 1985) suggest that the content of school subjects may be highly unpredictable in its effects on different pupils. Furthermore, such content may not be understandable by any critique based on charges that the content lacks relevance or realism. We would have to consider instead how children from various cultural, geographical and economic backgrounds can locate themselves in the different narratives found within the school subjects, and whether they accept, reject or re-interpret the positions offered them as learners.

Third, following on from this, we must ask what the form and content of curricula do for us, the adults and teachers, and what is involved in the production of curriculum materials for children. Jacqueline Rose's work on Peter Pan (1984) looked at the psychological functions which may be served by writing fiction for children, but, as far as I am aware, similar issues have rarely been explored in the study of non-fiction elements of the curriculum. In my own study of earlier history and geography books for younger children it was difficult to avoid the conclusion that writing and using these books secured for adults a world safely ordered both in time and space. Among more recent attempts to teach children about industry there is evidence of the way in which making economic matters amenable to the children can also make them acceptable to the adults. In some reports on industry projects in primary schools, for example (Jamieson, 1985; Smith, 1986; Smith, 1988) the 'world of work' can appear re-possessed by adults in education, making it secure, integrated, rational and even playful.

If it is useful to consider why certain curriculum materials and programmes satisfy or appeal to teachers and other adults; it may also be important to look at what it is about the Wiener thesis itself, and others like it, which appeals to some politicians, industrialists, and some educationalists.

One could begin by seeing a similarity between the blaming of a nation's culture for its economic difficulties, and earlier attempts to blame the culture of working class parents for the comparative failure of their children in schools. Perhaps the national culture can be seen as deformed in the way that those parents' culture was deprived. As was so frequently pointed out at the time when cultural deprivation arguments were so popular, such ideas served only to re-direct attention away from the teachers and the schools at which these children so persistently failed. In a somewhat conspiratorial sense it is possible to argue that blaming the culture and, more specifically, the agencies of cultural transmission for economic problems was an excellent way for industrialists to defend their autonomy and freedom to carry on as before. John Beck has shown how, against a background of political attempts in the 1970s to make British industrialists more accountable to their employees and to the state, they turned such demands on to the teachers (Beck, 1983). In that paper it is also suggested how linking education to industrial policy had certain political advantages for the Labour Government of the time. It showed it to be doing something in response to attacks on education by the Conservatives, it had the appearance of an industrial strategy, and it could be held up as a significant area of co-operation between government, unions and employers. If there could be no co-operation on prices, incomes, or any other vital aspects of national economic regeneration or control, the Government could at least launch the Schools Council Industry Project.

Trying now to understand the continuing popularity of the cultural and educational explanations for national economic decline one can hardly refer to any fears by industrialists of losing their autonomy, or to the hopes of Government to preserve the vestiges of corporatism. Whether or not Beck's analysis was a correct assessment of the motivations of industrialists or Government at the time, much has happened since to make us re-consider the very central notions of a national economy and a national culture, both in those accounts which blamed the schools and culture for the decline and those which blamed British industrialists themselves. At a time when the economy seems to open, so easily influenced by the strength or weakness of the American dollar, so penetrated by manufactured imports, and so dependent on decisions by multi-national companies based both in the UK and elsewhere, the appeal of a thesis which keeps explanations of economic failure and future success within national boundaries is reassuring to many. Plus, when the explanation requires a revised national culture, enshrined, perhaps, in a national curriculum and prompted by the spread of enterprise initiatives, then it is truly comforting.

All the institutions of British capitalism are kept intact, along with their traditional interrelations. Continuity is ensured for long-held conceptions of the British national interest and status as a world power, and the only change envisaged is within peoples' attitudes and beliefs. In important respects national unity is secured; 'our problems' are 'our own fault' and the cure is 'within ourselves'. Educators are given a role for the future, but only just so long as they adopt and promote the values of enterprise, initiative and competitive individualism [. . .].

Returning now to education it is possible to use the debate surrounding criticisms and alternatives to cultural theories of economic decline to illuminate some dilemmas in developing a justifiable programme of industrial and economic awareness in primary schools. My point is, that it would be useful for those in education to take seriously current academic and political debate about the nature of Britain's economic decline and the policy alternatives developed from it. The reason is that popular educational innovations can fulfil only too easily the demands made upon educators by a flawed theory of economic failure, misunderstanding and over-inflating as it docs the cultural aspects at the cost of the institutional and political. It has to be admitted, however, that exploring the educational significance of the debate between different explanations of economic decline does produce some considerable difficulties for teachers working within the national school system.

It is clear from any consideration of educational discussion about industry in schools, especially when it is concerned with the earlier years, that few educationalists see their task as promoting pro-industrial attitudes in accordance with the demands of the cultural theory of economic decline, in spite of the fact that some of the political space and encouragement for such work may have been provided by those who would believe that theory. A full range of justifications can be found in the educational literature concerned with industrial awareness, and they include a concern to give children access to some crucial concepts necessary for a general economic understanding. To use a popular set of distinctions, there appears to be a much greater commitment to educating about industry and through industry *for* industry (Blyth, 1984; Smith, 1988). In a variety of surveys of primary school industry work, for example, and in the range of case studies reported in Smith (1988) and Waite (1986) it is clear that, within the schools at least, there are few who use the Wiener thesis to justify their work. Only rarely do we find explicit reference to overcoming anti-industrial attitudes and the primary schools role in such a cultural conversion (Mercer, 1988). More often than not the programmes are presented as introductions to 'the world of work' and the means of breaking down what are seen as unnecessary barriers between schools and the real world. That world, it is argued, should be appropriated and opened up for children, and industrial topics can help them relate aspects of what they learn in school to the world outside the classroom (Smith, 1988, p. 10). Because it is in some sense 'real' then the world of work is thought to be likely to stimulate a whole range of communication, language, social and other skills which an isolated schooling can suppress.

When attempts are made to strengthen the structure of industrial and/or economic awareness then the concepts mentioned are derived from both sociology and neo-classical economics. In *Looking at the World of Work* (Ross and Smith, 1985) we find the concepts of co-operation, interdependence, division of labour and authority, along with capital, value, price etc. A similar list was incorporated into the Inner London Education Authority guidelines on social studies (ILEA, 1981). This combination of concepts from two different academic subjects means that children could be seen as both learning how industry fits with other spheres of activity, as well as coming to be aware of the nature of the social world and the range of social relations found there.

With such a spread of justifications one cannot complain that children are being made uncritically appreciative of industrial enterprises, or that they are necessarily being given one-sided views of employment. 'Work' is defined as broad enough to include consideration of state institutions as well as trades unions disputes and the range of concepts used would not exclude consideration of co-operative forms of enterprise. What is interesting from the point of view of this paper is that these rationales, and the examples of practice, are all *congruent* with the Wiener thesis, although, clearly, not the products of it. As *educational* justifications for a certain addition to the primary school curriculum they are quite consistent with a recent political strategy for bringing industry into education, culminating with the *Enterprise and Education Initiative* in 1988. In turn, the political rhetoric of putting schools in close contact with industry is consistent with, if not actually derived from a belief that future economic success depends on an assault being made on the assumed anti-industrial bias of our educational institutions. It is not that these two consistencies are rationally or conspiratorially linked, but what is noteworthy is what is excluded in both. There is little possibility within these consistent rhetorics of equipping pupils with any of the concepts or general understandings necessary to deal with the *politics* of industrial and economic development. Without a serious consideration of some ways of introducing young people to the political-institutional contexts in which economic enterprises work, many future citizens will be unable to address economic issues politically, but only as consumers, workers, owners or dependents. The tendency in contemporary projects on the world of work, mini-enterprises, local school-industry links, and other initiatives, is to give children an often excellent insight into the technical functioning and social life of a company, but either to present it in isolation or, at best, to insert it in a rather abstract environment of trade, exchange or society.

To avoid reiterating the criticisms already made about the absence of any political and social education with the youth, there are vocational programmes at the other end of the school system (see, for example, Gleeson 1985). I want to explore the particular difficulties of introducing to younger pupils a central family of concepts for contemporary citizenship when linked with industrial or economic awareness.

One of the difficulties of even starting to equip young people with the conceptual tools for citizenship arises, not because of the problems associated with teaching so-called controversial issues, but because there is a conceptual hole in the very middle of contemporary educational discussion about political, economic and social education itself. That hole is the space which was once occupied by 'the nation' in the conventional history and geography curriculum. As Jeffs points out, after the Second World War opposition to political education was much less pronounced because it was thought that any development of political or social awareness would necessarily preserve and further 'the British way of life' (Jeffs, 1988, p. 29). Since the 1960s however, because of various social changes and because of the nationalist and racist overtones in the ways 'the nation' had been presented to children, there has been a certain lack of frankness about the fact that at least some conception of 'the nation', some ability to apply the adjective 'national', is necessary to gain entry to most contemporary political and economic debates. Our discussion of theories of economic decline is but an illustration of this. Yet for a whole variety of reasons many educators in Britain have become extremely ambivalent about this concept and have tended to allow what are often their Right wing critics to articulate it as a cultural and sometimes political-racial unit.

Exactly what are the difficulties in attempting to introduce children to some conception of the national which would be useful for political and economic understanding? Again one is forced to use words like congruence and consistency to present the relationship between some contemporary educational and some political and economic discourse. On one side is a child-centred discourse which has its roots in both an anti-nationalism and anti-militarism of the founders of progressive education (viz., Selleck, 1972) and the developmentalism of Piaget. On the other are a series of actual and theoretical developments which have cast doubt on the possibility of a national economy, or the state as a legitimate economic force.

Some research in the developmental tradition would certainly discourage teachers from believing that they could get very far with developing any sense of nation, society or community during the primary state of schooling. For example, Jahoda's original work with 6 to 11-year-olds (1963, 1964) could be taken as showing that young children had little conception of nation until 11 years of age, at least when asked some oddly fundamental questions as 'What is Britain?'

This is not the place to enter the complex debates about the methodological, epistemological and ontological pre-suppositions in Piagetian research. In the end all such development studies can show is, not that children *cannot* learn about these things, but that they do not, naturally, enter such conceptual worlds.

Many teachers have now become more aware of the problems of much Piagetian work in this field but there is another, related aspect of contemporary educational discourse which may make for difficulties in developing satisfactory initiatives in political–economic education. The dual emphasis on realism and experience can make it very difficult to explore with children the *inter-institutional* relations of an economic and political kind. Visits to *real* factories, depending on children's actual experience of shops and the local environment, or even giving them the experience of running their own mini-enterprise, may well produce pedagogic contexts which make it particularly hard to learn about the inter-institutional economic relationships within a given space or between different societies. This does not imply that children would have to be taught exclusively by a direct pedagogy when such issues were covered, but it is likely that inter-institutional relations could be better explored in 'unrealistic' settings. Such artifical contexts, simple models of contemporary communities, for example, complete with institutions of consumption and production, could be produced in such a way that there was a lower density of experiential reference. Here the 'realism effect' could depend more upon the children being involved in narratives or identifying with a position in the setting from which they could make calculations and play roles.

Another reason why it seems so difficult for teachers in state schools to deal with that group of political and economic concepts concerned with state and nation is that the previous conventions of representing 'the nation' to children now seem so contradicted by contemporary ideological, political and economic developments. Recent discussion about the nature of the national history curriculum have shown the depth and range of objections to any return to a representation of the past as the unfolding of a unified, national essence (Samuel, 1989a). The publication of three volumes on the nature of British patriotism can only help to heighten our sensitivity to the gross pitfalls of naïveté which threaten any attempts to represent 'the nation' in schools (Samuel, 1989b). The dangers are clear, but missing in most of this debate has been a consideration of how one could now represent national economic space, and how one could legitimately present notions, however simple, of the national and international economy. The matter is of some significance not least because a nationalist and over-inflated view of Britain may well have made its own contribution to post-war decline, causing over-expenditure on the military (Chalmers, 1985) and pretensions about the value of sterling (Hall, 1987).

In the past representations of the internal national economy have been confused with the attempted construction of cultural Englishness. Where reference was made to national economic space, it was shown to children as an interlocking system in which different regions or towns made their distinctive contributions to national wealth (Ahier, 1988, pp. 127–132). Children could learn that there were, within a coherent national economy, different places providing different, tangible goods—steel in Sheffield, engines in Coventry, and so on. Viewed externally the image of the economy in school texts has been in terms of what it exports and imports. When the history of the national economy has been outlined, there has been very little on structures or institutions. Oddly, the only genuine attempts to present children with the rudiments of a political–economic history were in the representations of the feudal village. Even books for very young children have included references to ownership, class, exchange, surplus and rent (Ahier, 1988 p. 116). Capitalist agriculture, however, was usually described as the development of technologies only, and the growth of industry has excluded concern for banks, borrowing, saving, the formation of companies or trade unions.

Clearly all these representations are now inadequate. Not only was the image of Britain as the workshop of the world finally laid to rest in 1983 when the United Kingdom became a net importer of manufactured goods, but the last fifteen years of de-industrialization, however explained, have had such differential effects on the regions and cities of Britain that links between localities and specific product have been, for the most part, destroyed. Old notions of the nation exporting those categories of goods which were in surplus, and importing those which were needed, are also outdated because the openness of the economy and the dominance of the multinational companies has developed two-way in similar products. However, the ultimate question is whether the difficulty in representing the national economy to future citizens stems from the fact that such a concept is now completely redundant.

Arguments to show the demise of national economies come from both the political Right and Left, partly as reactions to the declared failure of the Keynesian policies of the post-war period. To some on the Right, notions of a national economy conjure up thoughts of closed, state-dominated systems, thought to be crumbling all over the world in the face of economic liberalism and the urge of all people to be 'free'. Redwood's Popular Capitalism, for example (Redwood, 1988), traces the spread of privatization, the growth of stock markets, and other signs of the flowering of enterprise as a global phenomenon, undermining previous notions of states as economic units. Those of another political persuasion refer to the evolution of a world system and argue that global capitalism is so pervasive and now so organized that what happens in any given state is determined by the world system (Wallerstein, 1974).

Whatever political stance one adopts it has to be admitted that certain developments do appear to have, at least, undermined the autonomy of national economies in general and the British economy in particular. Besides the obvious effects of international agencies like the World Bank and the International Monetary Fund, and the present movement of the European Economic Community towards monetary union, two changes above all appear to destroy the integration of the national economy. First there has been the growth in importance of foreign-owned companies operating within Britain, and in the foreign operations of British companies. Four hundred and two of the 1,000 largest companies in the UK are foreign owned, employing one in seven British workers. In 1983, 70 of the leading British manufacturing multi-nationals produced more in their foreign operations than they did at home, and for nine years they had increased employment in their overseas subsidiaries as they cut employment at home (Stopford and Turner, 1985, pp. 3–13). The importance of these facts for a concept of the national economy is clear if one considers the recent difficulties the Monopolies and Mergers Commission has had over attempting to define 'the national interest' when it tried to deal with foreign company buy-outs.

Another, although not separate problem in conceptualizing the national economy stems from the ease with which the new international financial markets encourage capital to flow in and out. Again, given the analysis of the City provided by Ingham and others, it is probably that Britain is particularly open to this development and the openness is further accentuated by recent changes in technology and a deliberate erosion of national controls through de-regulation. Not only may this undermine the degree to which Britain can pursue a whole range of policies for industrial regeneration, but the significance of the financial market can have geo-political effects. Massey, for example (1988) has argued that, because of the concentration of the finance sector in London, its local economy and that of a whole surrounding area is more linked to other international metropolitan regions and world cities than the rest of the United Kingdom. At the very least the scale of capital flows has shaken any belief that the symbol of the national economy, its currency, can be tightly controlled for the purposes of national economic management.

For these, and many other reasons, it could be concluded that, at best, the UK is but the site for the playing out of international forces. Any notion of a national organization of the economy, or even the possibility of an influence on that economy by citizens via their political representatives, can be regarded as an outdated mirage which passed with the end of corporatism. To educators working in an educational system, which itself is becoming less economically integrated as a result of the Education Reform Act, then notions of a national political-economic system may seem particularly out of date. An educational implication of this might be that within a de-nationalized market environment it would be quite adequate for children to acquire skills in personal money management, to have some experience of the work places in which they may, one day find themselves, to appreciate the inexorable rules of profit and loss, and then to cover any development of citizenship via a skills-oriented programme in personal and social education.

However, there are grounds for suspecting that news of the demise of national economies has, in fact, been grossly exaggerated. For some on the political Right the exaggeration has been used to convince employees that the state can no longer protect them from international competition. For some on the Left the idea of global capital moving to whichever place can provide the cheapest labour can be used to show workers the illusion of social democratic and Keynesian solutions (Radice, 1984). It is noteworthy that many of the arguments about the disappearance of national economies tend to concentrate only on the large multi-nationals, over emphasizing their global co-ordination and pursuit of cheap labour (Gordon, 1988). Even if multi-national companies are difficult to influence directly via national policies, they are not impervious, for they must still respond to national conditions which could, to some extent be controlled. (For a discussion of this viz., Tomlinson, 1988). Certainly it would be a mistake to ignore smaller companies and their inter-relations within national boundaries which could be influenced by both national and even local economic policies. To accept that the old means of controlling the economy via direct state nationalization or control of capital movement would now be very difficult is not to deny that the possibility of new institutional means of influencing or even supplementing markets are possible, and, in the UK, necessary.

Those arguing that national economies no longer exist often depend on ideas about universal changes in production and organization, but such changes do not all point in the same direction. Indeed, some features in the development of flexible production, such as so-called 'just-in-time' sourcing, may produce a greater integration and hence be more territorially specific. Thus it could be the case that contemporary developments do not necessarily diminish the significance of national strategies and policies, even though internationalization and openness may produce new constraints. The problem might well lie more in the way contemporary popular political-economic debate has been forced into the simple conflict between state and market solutions in Britain's economic problems.

However, even if it could be established that, for an economically aware citizenship, some general conception of the national economy is both possible and desirable this does not require that children should be taught about multi-national companies or the flows of capital. All that is implied is that the initial stages in an education for economic awareness should set the scene for some comprehension of economic activity at the institutional and national levels. Regardless of the academic problems of defining the national economy, almost every day, children are surrounded by extraordinary images of it in the mass media which any education for citizenship could not avoid, and should not leave undisturbed.

Over the last twenty years, at least, representations of that national economy have been at the very heart of political conflict and remain fundamental in the struggle for votes and political dominance. There have been all manner of corporal metaphors; bodies with cancers and sickness; creatures drunk on inflation. More recently there have been re-births and robust constitutions which are 'fundamentally sound'. In its own way the popular press has pampered and sustained the economically illiterate citizen. On August 24, 1989, as they reported the second largest trade deficit in Britain's history, and that for the first time, imports had exceeded ten billion pounds a month, the media managed to make a long-term deterioration in the balance of payments sound like a sudden, unexpected 'plunge' (*The Sun*). *The Daily Star*, *The Daily Express* and the *Daily Mirror* could all identify the culprits, however. In the first it was 'Snobby motorists', who 'stampeded to snap up the latest vehicles from abroad'. The *Express* blamed what was, in fact, a brief and insubstantial dock strike, and in the editorial of the *Mirror*, responsibility fell on one person, the Chancellor. In most of the papers, those who suffered were 'us'—ordinary British homeowners who, privately, would have to carry the burden via high mortgage rates. In the light of these representations some long-term development of a national political economic awareness needs no further justification.

The problem as to how this could be started at the earlier stages of schooling is not insoluble. One does not have to return to old, over-integrated representations of the nation to develop some understanding of the inter-relations between economic and other institutions with a given space. But nor should schools further accentuate contemporary disintegrative and unequal trends by avoiding the national picture, or just leaving it to the teaching of a national history. Perhaps the greatest danger is that of localism. Economic awareness projects which only consider local places of work in large areas of the South of England, for example, might well serve to sustain a currently popular underestimation there of the significance of manufacturing for the balance of payments and the future of employment. If local enterprises are studied they should then be related to the local and national economy in which they exist. Similarly, if mini-enterprises are used to further economic understanding, then the participants could be encouraged to explore the effects on their enterprises of different national or international economic and political conditions. Changes in contexts could be fed into the projects forcing inter-institutional considerations.

Yet, even after patient work on developing and researching a variety of approaches to economic awareness in the early years of schooling and beyond, those involved may still face a larger, less specific difficulty—that the world of children and the world of the economy are contradictorily related. On the one hand there are considerable pressures to keep children and their family life isolated from the world of work and political and economic calculation. On the other, children are mercilessly initiated into consumerism. They are, themselves, inveterate little consumers of imported goods. The UK toy sector of the economy, like others, saw a drop in the balance of its trade, from a surplus of £22 million in 1978 to a deficit £245 million in 1988 (Garnett, 1989). They are also used by advertisers, employers and other adults as the objects of economic effort and the beneficiaries of domestic credit. Schools, too, play their part, as the place where fashion is followed and comparisons made. Thus children, and their families, are necessary economic subjects, but in a private world, and attempts to develop a political–economic education can so often be seen as an affront to that privacy. In the end it is this which could defeat attempts to develop an economic awareness useful for citizens and not just comforting for adults.

Notes

1. For a full account of these images within textbooks see Ahier, 1988.
2. The same heroes of the industrial revolution continue to be referred to in similar ways, and are now held up to children as examples of enterprise. Duynrowse and Elliot, in their foreword to Smith's *Industry in the Primary School Curriculum* (1988) write as follows, 'Our late Georgian and Victorian forebears had enterprise in abundance. Men like Josiah Wedgwood, George Stephenson, Michael Faraday—most of them with little more than a rudimentary formal education behind them—accelerated the transformation of a largely agricultural and occasionally starving country into a society capable of providing high living standards and economic freedom for a vast majority of its members'. (p. xi).
3. This term is being used here only to distinguish those who identify the institutions of British economic and political life as the major sources of the problem of comparative economic decline. It is not used in the more commonly restricted sense to refer to those who necessarily follow the so-called institutionalist school represented by the work of Piore and Sabel on Post-Fordism (1984).

References

Ahier, J. (1983) History and sociology of educational policy, in Ahier, J. and Flude, M. (eds) *Contemporary Education Policy*, Croom Helm, Beckenham.
Ahier, J. (1988) *Industry, Children and the Nation*, Falmer Press, London.
Anderson, P. (1964) Origins of the present crisis, *New Left Review*, **23**.
Anderson, P. (1968) Components of the national culture, *New Left Review*, **50**.
Barratt Brown, M. (1988) Away with all the great arches: Anderson's history of British capitalism, *New Left Review*, **167**.
Beck, J. (1983) Accountability, industry and education, in Ahier, J. and Flude, M. (eds) *Contemporary Education Policy*, Croom Helm, Beckenham.
Berti, A. and Bombi, A. (1988) *The Child's Construction of Economics*, Cambridge University Press, Cambridge.
Best, M. H. (1989) Sector strategies and industrial policy; the furniture industry and the Greater London Enterprise Board, in Hirst, P. and Zeitlin, J. (eds) *Reversing Industrial Decline?*, Berg, Oxford.
Blyth, W. (1984) *Industry, education: case studies from the North West*, in Jamieson, I. (ed.) *We Make Kettles: Studying Industry in the Primary School*, Longman and School Council, London.
Carrington, B. and Troyna, B. (1988) *Children and Controversial Issues*, Falmer, Lewes.
Chalmers, M. (1985) *Paying for Defence: Military Spending and British Decline*, Pluto Press, London.
Coates, D. and Hillard, J. (1986) *The Economic Decline of Modern Britain*, Wheatsheaf Books, Brighton.
Coward, R. (1977) Class, 'culture' and the social formation, *Screen*, 18.1.
Crouzet, F. (1985) *The First Industrialists: The Problem of Origins*, Cambridge University Press, Cambridge.
Elbaum, B. and Lazonick, W. (1986) *The Decline of the British Economy*, Clarendon Press, Oxford.

Fletcher, C. and Kipling, R. (1911) *A School History of England*, Oxford University Press, Oxford.

Frith, G. (1985) 'The time of your life': the meaning of the school story in Steedman, C., Urwin, C., and Walkerdine, V. (eds) *Language, Gender and Childhood*, Routledge and Kegan Paul, London.

Frobel, F., Heinrichs, J. and Dreye, O. (1980) *The New International Division of Labour*, Cambridge University Press, Cambridge.

Furth, H. (1978) Young childen's understanding of society, in McGurk, H. *Issues in Childhood Social Development*, Methuen, London.

Garnett, N. (1989) Manufacturers play tough for survival in toytown, *Financial Times*, 12.8.89.

Gleeson, D. (1985) Privatisation of industry and the nationalisation of youth, in Dale, R. (ed.) *Education Training and Employment*, Pergamon Press, Oxford.

Gordon, D. M. (1988) The global economy: new edifice or crumbling foundations?, *New Left Review*, **168**.

Gunn, S. (1988) The 'failure' of the Victorian middle class; a critique, in Wolff, J. and Seed, J. (eds) *The Culture of Capital*, Manchester University Press, Manchester.

Hall, J. (1987) The State, in Causer, G. (ed.) *Inside British Society*, Wheatsheaf Books, Brighton.

Hirst, P. and Zeitlin, J. (1989) *Reversing Industrial Decline?*, Berg, Oxford.

Howe, A. (1984) *The Cotton Masters, 1830–60*, Oxford University Press, Oxford.

Ingham, G. (1984) *Capitalism Divided? The City and Industry in British Social Development*, Macmillan, Basingstoke.

Ingham, G. (1988) Commercial capital and British development: A reply to Michael Barrat Brown, *New Left Review*, **172**.

Inner London Education Authority (1981) *Social Studies in the Primary School*.

Jahoda, G. (1963) The development of children's ideas about country and nationality, *British Journal of Educational Psychology*, **33**, 47–60, 143–53.

Jahoda, G. (1964) Children's concepts of nationality: a critical study of Piaget's stages, *Child Development*, **35**.

Jamieson, I. (1984) 'We Make Kettles': Studying Industry in the Primary School, Longman and School Council, London.

Jamieson, I. (1985) *Industry in Education*, Longman, Harlow.

Jeffs, T. (1988) Preparing young people for participatory democracy, in Carrington, B. and Troyna, B. (eds) *Children and Controversial Issues*, Falmer, Lewes.

Lorenz, E. (1989) The search for flexibility: Subcontracting networks in French and British engineering, in Hirst, P. and Zeitlin, J. (eds) *Reversing Industrial Decline?*, Berg, Oxford.

Marsland, D. (1988) *Seeds of Bankruptcy*, The Claridge Press, London.

Massey, D. (1988) Uneven development: social change and spatial division of labour, in Massey, D. and Allen, J. (eds) *Uneven Re-development*, Hodder and Stoughton, London.

Mathieson, M. and Bernbaum, G. (1988) The British disease: a British tradition?, *British Journal of Educational Studies*, **xxvi**, 2.

Mercer, D. (1988) Economic awareness in the primary school, *Education*, 3–13, 16, 1.

Midwinter, E. (1971) Curriculum and the E.P.A. community school, in Hooper, R. (ed.) *Curriculum, Context, Design and Development*, Oliver and Boyd, Edinburgh.

Newton, S. and Porter, D. (1988) *Modernisation. The Politics of Industrial Decline in Britain Since 1900*, Unwin Hyman, London.

Piore, M. and Sabel, C. (1984) *The Second Industrial Divide: Prospects for Prosperity*, Basic Books, New York.

Pollard, S. (1982) *The Wasting of the British Economy, 1945 to the Present*, Croom Helm, London.

Radice, H. (1984) *The national economy: a Keynesian myth?* Capital and Class, 22.

Redwood, J. (1988) *Popular Capitalism*, Routledge, London.

Rose, J. (1984) *The Case of Peter Pan*, Macmillan, London.

Ross, A. Studying the world of work: an inevitable controversy, in Carrington, B. and Troyna, B. (eds) *Children and Controversial Issues*, Falmer, Lewes.

Ross, A. and Smith, D. (1985) *Schools and Industry, 5–13; looking at the world of work: Questions teachers ask*, Schools Industry Project.

Rostow, W. (1960) *The Stages of Economic Growth*, Cambridge, London.

Samuel, R. (1989a) New histories for old, in *History, The Nation and the Schools-Working Papers*, Ruskin College.

Samuel, R. (1989b) *Patriotism*, 3 vols., Routledge, London.

Selleck, R. (1972) *English Primary Education and the Progressives, 1914–1939*, Routledge and Kegan Paul, London.

Sked, A. (1987) *Britain's Decline*, Blackwell, Oxford.

Smith, D. (1986) *Industry Education in the Primary School*, School Curriculum Industry Project.

Smith, D. (1988) *Industry in the Primary School Curriculum*, Falmer Press, Lewes.

Stanworth, P. and Giddens, A. (1974) *Elites and Power in British Society*, Cambridge University Press, Cambridge.

Stopford, J. and Turner, L. (1985) *Britain and the Multi-nationals*, John Wiley, Chichester.

Thompson, E. (1965) The peculiarities of the English, in Miliband, R. and Saville, J. (eds) *The Socialist Register*.

Thompson, F. (1984) English landed society in the nineteenth century, in Thane, P., Crossick, G. and Floud, R. (eds) *The Power of the Past*, Cambridge University Press, Cambridge.

Tomlinson, J. (1988) *Can Governments Manage the Economy?*, Fabian Tract No. 524.

Waite, P. (1986) *Primary Schools and Industry in 1986, a report on the Industry Year workshops*.

Walkerdine, V. (1984) Developmental psychology and the child-centred pedagogy; the insertion of Piaget into early education, in Henriques, J., Holloway, W., Urwin, C., Venn, C. and Walkerdine, V., *Changing the Subject*, Methuen, London.

Wallerstein, I. (1974) *The Modern World System*, 2 vols., Academic Press, New York.

Wiener, M. (1981) *English Culture and the Decline of the Industrial Spirit, 1850–1980*, Cambridge University Press, Cambridge.

Wolff, J. and Seed, J. (1988) *The Culture of Capital*, Manchester University Press, Manchester.

Wrigley, J. (1986) Technical education and industry in the nineteenth century, in Elbaum, B. and Lazonick, W. (eds) *The Decline of the British Economy*, Clarendon Press, Oxford.

Zeitlin, J. and Totterdill, P. (1989) Markets, technology and local intervention; the case of clothing, in Hirst, P. and Zeitlin, J. (eds) *Reversing Industrial Decline?*, Berg Oxford.

Index